2015 Soonja Kwon

포엠포엠
POEMPOEM

천개의 눈물
A Thousand Tears
一千粒の涙

포엠포엠 시인선 011

권순자 한·영·일 대역 시집

Soonja Kwon's Korean, English, Japanese three languages bilingual collection of poems

- 韓国語、英語、日本語三ヶ国語対訳詩集 -

천개의 눈물
A Thousand Tears
一千粒の涙

Soonja Kwon 권순자

POEMPOEM

시인의 말

'꽃을 잊어버린 70년'의 소녀들이 있다.
짝사랑 고백도 못해보고 일본군을 몸으로 받아내야 했던 16세 소녀들이 있다.

어린 나이에 제2차 세계대전 일본군 부대로 끌려가서 꽃망울을 피어보지 못하고 고초를 겪은 처절한 아픔을 품고 연로하신, 할머니들이 병석에 들거나 소천하시는 것을 보고 더 이상 머뭇거릴 수 없었다. 티끌이라도 위로와 용기를 드리기 위해서 시를 쓰기 시작했다. 그 분들의 육신이 더 이상 이곳에 머물지 못할지라도 후손이 잊지 않고 그 뜻을 기리는데 한 몫을 하고 싶은 염원을 시집에 담았다.

이 시집은 일본군에 강제로 연행되거나 납치되어 일본군의 성노예로 고통스런 삶을 살았던 한국의 어린 소녀들에 대한 기록을 바탕으로 한, 일본군의 만행을 고발하는 시집이다. 시집을 통해서 그 소녀들의 상처를 위무하고 일본정부의 진심어린 참회의 사과를 요구하며, 조속히 합당한 해결을 바란다. 그것은 가장 가까운 이웃나라 한국에 대한 일본의 예의이고 용기 있는 행동일 것이다.

2015년 8월
권 순 자

Author's Preface

There are girls who were robbed of their bloom and neglected for 70 years.

There are girls who never had a chance to fall in love and who had to surrender their bodies to the Japanese army when they were 16.

When I thought about the hardships, the miserable agony that had been suffered by these innocent young girls, now elderly ladies- many on their sickbeds or already dead, when they were forcibly taken for the Japanese Army troops in World War II, and denied the chance to experience the blossom of youth, I could hesitate no longer. Even though it is just a tiny gesture I started to write poems to give them a bit of comfort and courage. Even though some of them may no longer be here with us, in order that their descendants do not forget, I have tried to put my voice applauding their courage into this collection of poems.

This collection of poems was written to record a complaint against the barbaric acts committed by the Japanese army toward the young Korean girls who were forcibly hauled off or kidnapped to spend lives of miserable suffering while serving as sex slaves for the Japanese army. Through these poems I hope to soothe the wounds of those young girls and to demand an apology from the Japanese government, expressing their sincere repentance, along with arranging an appropriate settlement for these ladies, without any further delay. That is the most courteous and courageous thing Japan can do for its closest neighbor, Korea.

August 2015, Seoul
Soonja Kwon

『一千粒の涙』、詩人の言葉

「花を失った70年」の少女たちがいる。
　片想いの告白もしたことがなく、日本軍をその体で受けとめ、堪えなければならなかった16歳の少女たちがいる。

　幼い年にも関わらず、この少女たちは第2次世界大戦の際に日本軍部隊に連れて行かれ、つぼみから花を咲かせることもできず苦痛をなめた。その残酷な傷によって、少女たちは一生苦痛の中で過ごし、病床に入って年を取った後に亡くなるのを見て、これ以上躊躇することができなかった。ほんのわずかでも慰労と勇気を捧げるために詩を書き始めた。
　その方々の肉身がこれ以上ここに留まることができないとしても、子孫が忘れずにその気持ちを称えるのに役立てたいという念願を、この詩集に盛り込んだ。

　この詩集は日本軍に強制連行されたり、拉致されて日本軍の性奴隷になって苦しみの生を送った韓国の幼い少女たちに対する記録に基づいた、日本軍の蛮行を告発する詩集である。この詩集を通してその少女たちの傷を癒し、日本政府の誠意のこもった懺悔の謝罪を要求し、速やかにしかるべき解決を願う。それは最も近い隣りの国、韓国に対する日本の礼儀であり、勇気ある行動であろう。

2015年、8月
權順慈(クォン·スンジャ)

Contents

시인의 말 · 7
Author's Preface
『一千粒の涙』、詩人の言葉

위안부 1 · 14
Female Slave 1
慰安婦 1

위안부 2 · 20
Female Slave 2
慰安婦 2

위안부 3 · 26
Female Slave 3
慰安婦 3

위안부 4 — 납치 1 · 32
Female Slave 4 — Kidnapping 1
慰安婦 4 — 拉致 1

위안부 5 — 납치 2 · 38
Female Slave 5 — Kidnapping 2
慰安婦 5 — 拉致 2

위안부 6 · 44
Female Slave 6
慰安婦 6

위안부 7 · 48
Female Slave 7
慰安婦 7

위안부 8 · 54
Female Slave 8
慰安婦 8

위안부 9 — 정서운(鄭書云) · 60
Female Slave 9 — Jeong Seowoon
慰安婦 9 — 鄭書云(ジョン・ソウン)

위안부 10 · 66
Female Slave 10
慰安婦 10

위안부 11 · 72
Female Slave 11
慰安婦 11

위안부 12 — 강제연행 1 · 76
Female Slave 12 — Forced Haul 1
慰安婦 12 — 強制連行 1

위안부 13 — 강제연행 2 · 82
Female Slave 13 — Forced Haul 2
慰安婦 13 — 強制連行 2

위안부 14 — 강제연행 3 · 86
Female Slave 14 — Forced Haul 3
慰安婦 14 — 強制連行 3

위안부 15 — 김달선 · 92
Female Slave 15 — Kim Dal-seon
慰安婦 15 — 김달선(キム・ダルソン)

위안부 16 — 김연희 · 98
Female Slave 16 — Kim Yeon-hee
慰安婦 16 — 김연희(キム・ヨンヒ)

위안부 17 — 환생 · 104
Female Slave 17 — Reincarnation
慰安婦 17 — 転生

고마워요 · 110
Thank You
ありがとうございます

증언 1 · 114
Witness 1
証言 1

증언 2 · 120
Witness 2
証言 2

증언 3 · 126
Witness 3
証言 3

기도 · 132
Prayer
祈り

편지 · 138
Letter
手紙

위안소 여자의 독백 · 144
Soliloquy of a Female Slave
慰安所の女の独白

천개의 눈물 · 148
A Thousand Tears
一千粒の涙

증언 4 · 154
Witness 4
証言 4

봄 처녀 · 158
Spring Maiden
春の娘

팔라우 섬 한인 소녀 · 162
Korean Girls on the Islands of Palau
パラオ島の韓国人少女

콰이강의 다리 · 168
The Kwai River Bridge
クウェー川の橋

아, 라멍 라멍 ― 증거인멸 · 174
Ah, Ramung, Ramung ― Vanishing Proof
ああ!ラモウ、ラモウ ― 証拠隠滅

천개의 눈물
A Thousand Tears
一千粒の涙

위안부 1

> 일본군 위안부 피해자
> 할머니가 별세했다

돌아보고 싶지 않구나
생각하고 싶지도 않구나
그래도 악몽은 발뒤꿈치 들고
어둠보다 재빨리 와서 잠을 방해하는구나

전쟁은 공포스러웠어
밤은 더 무서웠어

달이 피를 흘리는 걸 보았니
달빛이 핏줄기로 쏟아지는 것을 본 적 있니
나의 달은 낮이고 밤이고 피를 흘렸어
눈물대신 피가 흘렀고
콧물대신 피가 흘렀어
아랫도리도 피가 흘렀어

소리친다고?
소리치면 누가 와서 말려 줄 수 있어?

엄마는 너무 멀리 있고
나의 나라는 이름조차 빼앗겨
내가 어디서 죽어가는지도 몰랐어

전쟁괴물들만 득실거렸어

발목이 수십 수백 명의 감시줄에 걸려
그 욕된 막사를 도망치지 못했어

전쟁이 끝나도 머릿속이 지워지지 않았어

Female Slave 1

A brave old lady, who suffered
as a female slave, has passed away

I don't want to look back
I don't want to think about it
And yet the nightmares that haunt me
Come faster than the night and interrupt my sleep

The war was terrifying
The night even more terrifying

Did you see the moon shedding blood?
Have you seen the moonlight gushing streams of blood?
My moon has shed blood by day, by night
From my eyes poured not tears but blood
From nose what poured was blood
And from my nether parts the blood poured too

Did you say I should scream?
If I scream will somebody come to stop this?

Mom is too far away
My country has been stripped of its name
Have I died, so I can't remember what country I'm from?

Overwhelmed with the spectres of war

My ankle bound by dozens, hundreds of watchful eyes
I could not escape from that shameful barracks

Even though the war is over the memories do not vanish

慰安婦 1

> 日本軍慰安婦被害者である
> おばあさんが逝去した

振り返ってみたくない
考えたくもない
それでも悪夢はかかとをあげて
闇よりすばやくやって来て眠りを妨げる

戦争は恐ろしかった
夜はもっと怖かった

月が血を流すのを見たことがあるか
月の光が血潮になってほとばしるのを見たことがあるか
私の月は昼も夜も血を流した
涙の代わりに血が流れ
鼻水の代わりに血が流れた
下半身からも血が流れた

叫んだだって？
叫んだら誰かが来て止めてくれるの？

母はあまりに遠くにいて
わが国は名前さえ奪われて
私がどこで死んでいくのかも知らなかった

戦争の怪物たちだけがうようよしていた

足首は数十人、数百人の監視の縄に引っかかり
その侮辱の幕舎から逃げられなかった

戦争が終わっても頭の中のものは消えていない

위안부 2

이봐 우리가 승리하려면
군인들 힘 돋워야지
어디 조선여자들 데려와 봐.

도시 변두리나 시골에 가서
처녀들 집집마다 한 명씩 차출해서 데리고 와.

순사와 순사 앞잡이들 거동 보소

하, 일본순사한테 잘 보일 일 생겼네
이 동네 처녀들 많지

김씨네, 이씨네 열 서너 살 먹은 딸이 있지
뭐 별로 어렵지 않구먼

동민 여러분, 간호사를 모집합니다.
대우도 좋고 일도 어렵지 않습니다.
그 일이 힘들면 식당종업원 일도 있습니다.

가난한 딸들이 심청이 심정으로 집을 떠났다

여긴 병원이 아닌데
여긴 식당이 아닌데

열 서너 살 처녀들이
끌려간 간 곳은 환자가 기다리는 병원이 아니었다
음식을 조리하는 식당이 아니었다

군부대였다
도망갈 수도 없는,
죽고 싶어도 죽을 수 없는
전쟁터 위안소였다

속아서 끌려온 처녀들은
노예가 되었다

Female Slave 2

Look here, if we are going to win
We have to give the troops some strength
Go bring some of those Chosun girls.

Go to the countryside, to the outskirts of the cities
Recruit one girl from every house and bring them here.

The actions of those police officers and their spies will be recorded

Wow, what a lucky day for the Japanese patrols
This village has lots of young girls

There are Kims and Lees with daughters of 13 or 14
There's nothing difficult about it

Listen, everybody, we are looking for nurses
The salary is good, and the work is not hard.
If that work is too hard, we also need staff for the mess halls.

The poor girls leave home with the same heart as Shim Chung*

This is not a hospital
This is not a restaurant

These 13 and 14 year old girls
Were not taken to a hospital with waiting patients
Or a restaurant with food needing to be cooked

It was a military camp
No escape possible
Their battlefield where they couldn't die
Even when they wanted to
Was an army brothel.

Deceived and taken from home
The girls have become slaves

*Shim Chung is the heroine of an old Korean tale who sells herself into service as a sacrificial
 maiden for the money to donate to the temple and give her blind father his sight back.

慰安婦 2

おい、我々が勝つためには
軍人たちに力をつけるべし
さあ、朝鮮の女たちを連れて来い。

町の外れや田舎に行って
娘を家ごとに一人ずつ差し出させて連れて来い。

巡査と巡査の手下どもの挙動を見ろ

うん、日本の巡査におもねられる仕事が見つかったぜ
この町、生娘が多いだろ

金さんの家、李さんの家には 13、4歳の娘がいるだろ
何だ　そんなに難しくないぜ

町の皆さん、看護師を募集します。
待遇もいいし仕事も難しくありません。
その仕事が大変ならば食堂従業員の仕事もあります。

貧しい娘たちがシムチョン*の気持ちになって家を出た

ここは病院じゃないのに
ここは食堂じゃないのに

13、4歳の娘たちが
連れて行かれたところは患者の待つ病院ではなかった
食べ物を調理する食堂ではなかった

軍の部隊だった
逃げることもできない、
死にたくても死ぬことのできない
戦場の慰安所だった

騙されて連れて来られた娘たちは
奴隷になった

<訳者注>
*シムチョン(沈清)：朝鮮に古くから口伝で伝わる最古の民話『沈清伝』の主人公。「孝行沈清」と呼ばれる。

위안부 3

어머니
저는 언제 어머니를 볼 수 있을까요?

어머니를 위해서 고통을 참고 살았는데
저를 버리고 놈들이 도망을 가네요

아파서 걷지도 못하는 나를
흙구덩이에 던지고는 가버리네요

하늘이 너무 파랗군요
어머니 고향의 하늘도 새파란가요?

놈들이 흙을 마구 덮네요
어머니
저는 더 이상 어머니를 볼 수 없는 건가요?

돈을 준다더니 놈들은 돈도 떼먹고
나를 시체 버리듯이
먼 나라에 버리고 도망가네요

어머니라도 편안하게 해드려야 할텐데

어머니

너무 아파요
너무 서러워요
너무 무서워요
어머니 도와주세요

저 놈들을 용서하지 말아주세요
어머니!

Female Slave 3

Mother
I want to see you, Mother

I have gone through this pain for you, Mother
These guys have just thrown me here and fled

In too much pain to even walk
They threw my body in a hole in the ground and just ran

The sky is so beautiful and blue
Is the sky blue at home where you are, Mother?

Those guys have buried me alive
Mother
Won't I ever see you again?

They said they would pay me, but they keep all the money
And threw me away like I was dead
They threw me here in this far place, and they ran off

I should be there to help you, Mother

Mother

It hurts so much
I am so lonely
I am so scared
Mother, help me

Never forgive these bastards!
Mother!

慰安婦 3

お母さん
私はいつまたお母さんに会えるでしょうか。

お母さんに会うために苦痛をこらえて生きてきたのに
私を捨ててやつらは逃げて行きます

痛くて歩くこともできない私を
窪みに放り投げて行ってしまいます

空がとても蒼いです。
お母さんの故郷の空も真っ青ですか。

やつらがやたらに土を被せます
お母さん
私はもうお母さんに会えないのでしょうか。

お金をくれるっていったのにやつらはお金も踏み倒して
私を死体を棄てるように
遠い国に棄てて逃げて行きます

お母さんだけでも楽にしてあげなきゃいけないのに

お母さん

とても痛いです
とても恨めしいです
とても怖いです
お母さん、助けてください

あいつらを容赦しないでください
お母さん!

위안부 4
― 납치 1

나는 친구 집에 갔다가
돌아오는 길에
파출소 앞에서 순경에게 붙들렸다
간 곳이 위안소

어머니 제가 납치당했어요
어머니는 제가 어디로 갔는지도 모르죠

어머니 여기는 전쟁터에요
제가 위안부래요
제가 누구를 위안하는 것이죠?
저는 강제로 끌려온 노예인 걸요

제가 싫다고 여기를 벗어날 수도 없어요
죽기보다 싫어도 위안소를
벗어날 자유가 없어요

어머니 이 지옥을 벗어나고 싶어요
어제는 대들었다가 온몸이 피멍이 들었어요
아파도 울지 못해요

어머니
저는 이제 겨우 열다섯 살이에요

제가 무엇을 할 수 있을까요
힘도 없고 용기도 없어요

어머니 보고 싶어요
어머니 저를 찾아주세요
제발.

Female Slave 4
—Kidnapping 1

I was coming home
from my friend's house
passing by the police box and officer detained me
now I am at a an army brothel

Mother I have been kidnapped
Mother I have no idea where I am

Mother this is a battlefield
They call me a comfort girl
Who am I supposed to comfort?
Forced to come here I am a slave

I hate it here but I cannot leave
I have no freedom to leave
This army brothel that is worse than death

Mother I want to get away from this hell
Yesterday I complained so now I am covered with bruises
It hurts but I must not cry

Mother
I am only fifteen

Is there anything I can do
With no strength and no courage

Mother I want to see you
Mother come find me
I beg you.

慰安婦 4
― 拉致 1

私は友達の家に行って
帰り道に
交番の前でお巡りさんに捕まえられた
行った所が慰安所

お母さん 私は拉致されたんです
お母さんは私が何処に行ったのかも知らないでしょう

お母さん ここは戦場です
私が慰安婦だって
私が誰を慰安するのでしょうか
私は強引に引っ張って来られた奴隷なんです

私が嫌でもここから抜け出すこともできません
死ぬより嫌だと言っても慰安所を
抜け出す自由がありません

お母さん この地獄から逃れたいです
昨日たてついたら全身に青黒いあざを付けられました
痛くても泣くことができません

お母さん
私はまだやっと15歳です

私に何ができるのですか
力も無いし勇気もありません

お母さんに会いたい
お母さん 私を捜し出してください
後生だから。

위안부 5
— 납치 2

나는 어머니와 시장에서
생선을 팔고 있었어
일본군이 오더니 갑자기 나를 끌고 갔어
발버둥치고 울어도
나를 나무토막처럼 끌고 갔어

나는 전쟁터에 노예로 끌려간 거야
조선의 귀한 딸을
일본전쟁의 도구로 끌고 간 거야
열여덟 살 결혼할 처녀였는데.

수십 명, 수백 명 군인들의 노예로 살아야 했어
불쌍한 내 인생!
며칠 전까지
자유롭게 바닷가를 거닐었는데.
여기 날마다의 고통에
정신이 짓이겨지곤 했어

전쟁의 한가운데서 맞닥뜨린
몸서리치는 악몽이 현실이었어

죽음보다 두렵고
치욕스런 나날

고문의 순간들이
이어지고 기진하고 이어지곤 했어

나는 돌아갈 곳도 없어
만신창이 몸을 가누지도 못한 채
갈 곳을 잃었어.

악몽은 멈추지 않았어.

Female Slave 5
— Kidnapping 2

I was at the market
Selling fish with Mother
A Japanese soldier came and dragged me away
I struggled and screamed
But he dragged me off like a hunk of wood

Dragged to the battlefield now a slave
The precious daughter of my ancestors
A girl waiting to turn eighteen and marry
Now a Japanese instrument of war

I have to live as a slave for dozens, hundreds of soldiers
What a pitiful existence!
Until a few days before
I strolled carefree by the sea.
The agony of every day here
Crushes my spirit

In the middle of the war encountering
Reality that is a shuddering nightmare

More fearful than death
The disgrace of each day

The moments of torture
Continued, exhausted me and still continued

There is nowhere I can return to
My wreck of a body stands unsteadily
I do not know where to go

The nightmares do not end

慰安婦 5
── 拉致 2

私はお母さんと市場で
魚を売っていた
日本の軍人が来たと思ったらいきなり私を引きずって行った
あがいても泣いても
私を木切れのように引きずって行った

私は戦場に奴隷として引っ張って行かれたのだ
朝鮮の貴い娘を
日本の戦争の道具として引っ張って行かれたのだ
18歳、結婚するはずの娘だったのに。

数十人、数百人の軍人たちの奴隷として生きるしかなかった
哀れな私の人生！
何日か前まで
自由に海辺を歩き回ったのに。
ここでの日々の苦しさに
何度も精神が押しつぶされそうになった

戦争のど真ん中で突き当たった
身の毛のよだつ悪夢が現実だった

死よりも恐ろしく
恥辱の日々

拷問の瞬間が
続いて 気力が尽きてもまだ続いた

私は帰る場所もなく
満身創痍の体を支えられないまま
行き場所を失った。

悪夢は止まらなかった。

위안부 6

이상한 반장 아주머니였다
동네를 돌며 집집마다 딸 한 명씩
내놓으라는 것이었다

나는 식모로 있던 집의 딸을 대신해서
일본사람 따라서 기차를 탔다

군수물자 공장에서 며칠 일하다가
다시 배를 타고 어딘가로 끌려갔다

나는 사람이 아니었다
전쟁의 공포로 얼룩진 군인의
욕망을 받아주는 그릇이었다

나도 부잣집 딸이었다면 얼마나 좋았을까
따뜻한 집에서 부모와 살다가
남편 만나서 오붓하게 살 수 있었을 텐데

가난을 벗어나려 한 것이
목숨을 담보로 살아가는
노예가 되어버렸다

돈표는 받지도 못하고
병을 얻어 피폐한 나날을 살아간다

Female Slave 6

That strange village headwoman
came through the village asking for
one girl from every house

Just the housemaid, in place of their daughter
they sent me to take the train with that Japanese man

After working a few days in a munitions factory
Another boat took me away somewhere

I was no longer a person
But a vessel to receive all the desires
of soldiers stained by the terror of war

How I wished I were the daughter of a rich family
I would be living in a warm house with my parents
And starting a nice life with my husband.

Being stuck in poverty
My very life the only bargaining chip for survival
I have become a slave

Receiving no payment for my pains
Day by day sickness takes its toll

慰安婦 6

班長のおばさんは変だった
町中を回りながら家ごとに娘を一人ずつ
出せ、と言った

私は女中をしていた家の娘の代わりに
日本人に連れられて汽車に乗った

軍需品工場で数日か働いて
また船に乗せられて何処かへ引っ張られて行った

私は人間でなかった
戦争の恐怖にまみれた軍人たちの
欲望を受け止める器だった

私もお金持ちの娘だったらどんなによかっただろう
温かい家で両親と暮らして
夫に出会って一家団欒に暮らせただろうに

貧乏から抜け出すつもりが
命を担保にして生きてゆく
奴隷になってしまった

軍票はもらえもせず
病を得て荒んだ日々を生きている。

47

위안부 7

병이 걸렸다
군의관이 살바르산 주사를 놔주었다
어질어질하다

가끔씩 얼굴을 씰룩거리고 손을 떤다
임신방지하려고 강제로 수은증기를 쏘였을 거라고
옆에서 수군거린다

지겹다
줄지어선 군인들 보는 것도 끔찍하다
미리 고통이 상상되어서
숨이 멎는다

고통이여 멈추어다오

전쟁이 끝났다는 소식을 들었다
나는 고향을 떠올렸다.

고향이 그립지만
고향에 돌아가고 싶지 않다
만신창이 된 몸과 마음은
고향을 지워버렸다

나를 지워버리고 싶었다

나는 다시 꽃필 수 있을까
내가 다시 꽃으로 고와질 수 있을까
전쟁의 폐허 위에서?

Female Slave 7

I'm so sick
The army doctor gave me a shot of Salvarsan
I'm so dizzy

Sometimes my face quivers and my hands tremble
She's been mercurializing to keep from getting pregnant
They gossip about me in hushed voices

It is so disgusting
I cannot stand to even look at those lines of soldiers
Thinking about the pain that is coming
I can't even breathe

Make the pain stop

I heard that the war is over
I think about my hometown

I miss my home but
I don't want to go there
My mind and body ruined
I have erased my hometown

I wanted to erase myself

Can I bloom again?
Is it possible I can become a flower again
On top of the ruins of war?

慰安婦 7

病気にかかった
軍医がサルバルサンの注射を打ってくれた
めまいがする

時々顔がびくびくして手が振るえる
妊娠しないように強制的に水銀の蒸気を当てられたんだろうと
隣でこそこそ言っている

うんざりだ
列を作った軍人たちを見るのもぞっとする
前々から苦しみが想像されて
息が詰まる

苦しみよ、止まっておくれ

戦争が終わったという話を聞いて
私は故郷を思い浮かべた。

故郷が懐かしいが
故郷に帰りたくない
ぼろぼろになった肉体と心は
故郷を消してしまった

私を消してしまいたかった

私は再び花を咲かせられるのだろうか
私が再び綺麗な花になれるだろうか
戦争の廃墟の上で?

위안부 8

어째 구경만 하고 있는 건가?
배상금을 단 일 엔이라도 받아야겠어

전쟁을 일으키고
전쟁에 일반 부녀자를 강제로 끌고 갔으니
끌고 가서 노예로 삼았으니

당연히 배상을 해야 되는 것 맞지?
그런데 왜 말만 많은 건가?

네가 변명을 한다고 해서
내가 강제로 끌려가서 밤이고 낮이고
노예 생활한 사실이 사라지는 것인가?

네가 온갖 말로 덧칠하고 치장하고
지우려고 하더라도
너무 많은 기록들이 네 앞에 사라지지 않고
자꾸 새끼치고 있지

네가 한 마디 거짓말 하면
수많은 벌떼들이 숨어 있는 냄새를 파헤치지
벌들의 후각은 예민하고 정확해서
네가 입을 열어 거짓말을 할 때마다

수십 개, 수백 개의 증거들을 내놓지

네가
상해에서, 산동성에서, 나고야에서,
중국 무한에서, 오키나와에서,
미얀마와 중국 국경지대에서
파묻어버린 증거들이 부활해서
네 앞으로 성큼성큼 걸어가지.

파퓨아뉴기니에서의 학살장면까지,
중국과 미얀마 국경지대에서 발견된
위안부들의 시체 사진까지,
어린 처녀를 유괴, 납치한 사실까지

네가 가리면 가릴수록
악취 나는, 잔인한 행위의 자료들이
자꾸 자꾸 연기가 피어오르듯이
솟아나오지.

네 악취 나는 행동이 너를 삼켜버릴 때까지
나는 지켜보겠다
여기서 꼿꼿이 앉아서
저 하늘에 가서 꼿꼿이 굽어보면서.

Female Slave 8

How can you sit there and just watch what's going on?
You haven't given me even one Yen in compensation

You started a war
you took ordinary girls and dragged us to war
now we are all become slaves

You have to compensate us for this, don't you?
Why do you just avoid the issue and make excuses?

You say you have a reason.
Is there any way I will forget that I was
Forced to come be a slave night and day?

No matter how you try to dress it up or paint over it
Even if you try to wipe it out
All that is recorded about the slaves will never disappear
And new facts are coming out

If you tell even one lie
Countless swarms of bees will find the hidden scent
With their sensitive and accurate sense of smell
Every time your lips open to tell another lie
There will be dozens, hundreds of witnesses to the truth

All that you buried
from Shanghai to Shendong Province to Nagoya
from Wuhan, China to Okinawa
to the border area between China and Burma
every piece of hidden evidence will come to life
and appear before you one after another.

The massacre site in Papua New Guinea
and the photos of the bodies of dead female slaves
from the border area between China and Burma,
the kidnapping of young girls, the truth of their abduction

No matter how you try to cover up
the record of the stench of your brutal conduct
it will keep appearing like black smoke
that will never stop billowing out

Until the day that the stench of your actions swallows you up
I will keep my watch
Unyielding and glued to my seat
Or steadfastly watching you from heaven above

慰安婦 8

どうして見物ばかりしているのか
たったの1円でも賠償金をもらわねば

戦争を起こし
戦争に一般人の婦女子を強制的に引っ張って行ったから
引っ張って行って奴隷にしたから

賠償するのが当たり前だろう
なのにどうして口先ばかりなのか

お前がいくら弁解したとしても
私が強制的に引っ張られて行って夜も昼も
奴隷生活をした事実が消えるのか

お前があらゆる言葉で塗りたくり、うまく飾って
消そうとしても
あまりに多くの記録がお前の前から消えず
どんどん膨らんでいる。

お前が一言嘘をつけば
数多くの蜂の群れが隠された臭いを掘り返す
蜂たちの臭覚は鋭くて正確なので
お前が口を開いて嘘をつくたびに

数十、数百の証拠を立てる

お前が
上海で、山東省で、名古屋で、
中国の武漢で、沖縄で、
ミャンマーと中国の国境地帯で
埋めてしまった多くの証拠が蘇り
お前の前へつかつかと歩いて行くのだ。

パプアニューギニアでの虐殺シーンまで、
中国とミャンマーの国境地帯で発見された
慰安婦たちの死体の写真まで、
幼い娘たちを誘拐、拉致した事実まで

お前が隠せば隠すほど
悪臭のする、残酷な行為の多くの資料が
もくもくと煙が立ち上るように
溢れ出るのだ。

お前の悪臭のする行動がお前を呑み込んでしまうまで
私は見守るつもりだ
ここにしゃんと座って
あの天に昇ってもしゃんと見下しながら。

위안부 9
― 정서운 鄭書云

경남 하동에서 태어난 그는
18세 때 일본군 '위안부'로 끌려갔다.
인도네시아 스마랑에서 4년 동안
일본군 성노예 생활을 강요당하고, 22세에 해방을 맞았다.

해방 후 곧바로 집으로 돌아오지 못하고,
싱가포르 수용소에서 지내다 46년에 부산으로 귀국하였다.
그렇지만 이미 부모님은 사망하였고,
집은 폐허가 되어 할머니는 또다시 혼자여야 했다.

일본 순경에게 잡혀간 아버지

아버지, 제가 잡혀가면 아버지가 풀려난대서
이장 말 듣고 집을 떠났어요

제가 배를 타고 내린 곳은 일본이 아니었어요
인도네시아 스마랑
일본군대였어요

나는 발버둥치고 발악을 했어요
아편주사를 맞고 중독 되어서
결국 노예생활을 했어요
수많은 군인들, 군인들이 줄을 섰어요

아버지, 저는 죽고 싶었어요

말라리아 약 수십 알을 한꺼번에 삼켰어요
그래도 죽지 못했어요, 아버지
코로, 입으로, 온몸으로 피만 쏟아냈대요

일주일에 한번 씩 성병검사를 했어요

군용트럭을 타고 바깥병원에 갈 때면
길가의 인도네시아 원주민을 봤어요
얼굴이 새까만 그들이 반가워 눈물이 났어요

몸이 망가져도 다짐했어요
살아남아야 한다

일본군이 내 몸을 뺏어가도
내 마음까지는 안 뺏긴 거죠

전쟁이 끝나고 돌아왔어요, 아버지
제가 살아 돌아왔어요

그런데 아버지는 풀려나지 못하고
주재소에서 돌아가셨군요

아버지 집에 와서 아편을 끊었어요
죽을 만큼 괴로웠지만 끊었어요

아버지, 딸이 돌아왔어요

Female Slave 9
— Jeong Seowoon

Born in Hadong, South Gyeongsang Province and taken away to be a female slave when she was 18, for 4 years in Semarang, Indonesia she was forced to be a sex slave for the Japanese army, freed at 22.

After spending time in a Singapore prisoner of war camp she returned to Korea through Busan in 1946. But her parents were already dead, their house destroyed and she was alone again.

Father, the Japanese police took you away

Father, they said they will release you if I go with them
I left with them like the village headman said

But the boat didn't take me to Japan
It was Indonesia
Where the Japanese army is

I kicked and struggled
They shot me with opium and I got addicted
Finally I became their slave
So many soldiers, lines of soldiers waiting

Father, I wanted to die

I took handfuls of malaria pills
But I couldn't die, Father
I just bled from my nose, from my lips, from whole body

Tested every week for sexual diseases

They took me to the local hospital in the army truck
Along the road I saw the Indonesian people
Their sun-darkened faces brought tears of joy to my eyes

My body was bruised, but I was silent
My only focus was how to survive

Even though they stole my body
The Japanese army cannot have my mind

Father, the war is over and I came back
I lived, and I came back

But Father, they didn't release you
You died right there where you were

Father, I came home and stopped taking opium
It was agony, but I defeated the opium

Father, your daughter came home

慰安婦 9
― 鄭書云(ジョン・ソウン)

慶尚南道河東生まれの彼女は
18歳の時に日本軍「慰安婦」になって連れ去られた。
インドネシアのスマランで四年の間
日本軍の性奴隷の生活を強要され、22歳の時に解放を向かえた。

解放後はすぐ家に戻ることが出来ず、
シンガポールの収容所で過ごして、1946年に帰国して釜山へ帰った。
けれどもすでに両親は死亡しており、
家は廃虚となって老婆は再び一人ぼっちとなった。

日本巡査に捕まえられて行った父

お父さん、私が連れて行かれればお父さんが釈放されると聞いて
里長の話を信じて家を出ました。

私が船に乗って行って降りたところは日本ではありませんでした
インドネシアのスマラン
日本の軍隊でした

私は足をばたつかせて、暴れました
阿片の注射を打たれ、中毒にさせられ
その挙句、奴隷の生活をしました
数多くの軍人たち、軍人たちが列をつくりました

父さん、私は死んでしまいたかったです

抗マラリア剤を数十錠をまとめて呑み込みました
けれども死ねませんでした。お父さん
鼻から、口から、全身が血を吐き出したと後で聞きました

一週間に一回ずつ性病検査をされました

軍用トラックに乗って町の病院に行くときには
道端にいるインドネシアの原住民を見ました
顔の真っ黒な彼らに会えたのが嬉しくて涙が出ました

体がおかしくなっても心に決めました
生き残らなければと

日本軍が私の体を奪っても
私は心までは奪われませんでした

戦争が終わって帰ってきました、お父さん
私が生きて帰りました

けれどもお父さんは釈放されずに
駐在所で亡くなったのですね

お父さん、家に帰ってから阿片をやめました
死ぬほど苦しかったけれどもやめました

お父さん、あなたの娘が帰って来ました

위안부 10

몸이 짓밟힌
숨 막히는 막사에서
아, 밤이면
내 마음은 어디로 가는 걸까

고통과 불행의 배를 타고
허우적허우적
어디로 꿈을 꾸며 빠져나가는 걸까

울렁거리는 구토증을 쓸어내리며
방향을 잃고 기침하는 바람
슬픔으로 열렬한 몸을 두고
오오 마음이여
어디로 사라지려 하는가

악마의 소굴을 벗어나려고
절룩이며 헤매는 거친 맨발이여
칸칸이 박힌 울음과 신음의 물결이
막사를 떠돌고 꾸역꾸역
분노로 자라는가

잊지 말라
몸이 허물어지고 가라앉을지라도

정신은 선명하게 너의 행동을 각인하여
세상으로 끝없이 전송하는 것을

Female Slave 10

From these barracks where
my body is trampled and my breath choked
ah, when night comes
where does my spirit journey

On a boat of pain and misery
struggling
where do I escape in my dreams

Waves of nausea sweep over
losing my way in a coughing wind
leaving my body steeped in sorrow
O, my spirit
where will you disappear to?

To escape from Satan's den
wandering, passing on limping bare feet
From every room of the barracks
waves of cries and moans drift by me
my anger grows and grows

Never forget
Even if my body crumbles and sinks away

My spirit will bear clear witness to what you have done
Never ceasing I will proclaim it to all the world

慰安婦 10

体の踏みにじられた
息苦しい兵舎で
ああ、夜になると
私の心はどこに行くのか

苦痛と不幸の船に乗って
あっぷあっぷと
どこに夢見て抜け出すのか

むかむかする吐き気を撫で下ろしながら
方向を失って咳をする風
悲しみで熱くなった体を置いて
ああ、心よ
どこへ消え去ろうとするのか

悪魔の巣窟から抜け出すために
引き摺られつつ彷徨う荒れた素足よ
部屋ごとにめり込んだ泣き声と呻き声の波が
兵舎を漂ってむくむく
怒りに育つのか

忘れるな
体が崩れて沈んだとしても

精神は鮮明にお前の行動を刻印し
世界に終わりなく伝送するということを

위안부 11

뭐라구요?
강제연행이 아니었다구요?

공장 취직시켜준다고 해서 따라갔는데
배에서 내려준 곳이
인도네시아 일본전쟁터였잖아요?
전 열두 살이었어요
제 친구는 열다섯 살이었어요

그럼 제가 전쟁터
남자군인들이 수십 명 수백 명 줄 서서
성적욕구 풀려는 지옥의 전장에
제 발로 스스로 갔다구요?
전쟁과 참혹한 죽음을 시시때때로 겪는
군인들에게
성노예로 제가 알아서 갔다구요?

그곳이 공장이었나요?

당신 딸에게 물어보세요
당신의 열네 살 손녀에게 물어보세요

Female Slave 11

What did you say?
Nobody forced me to go there?

I went because they promised me a good factory job.
But didn't the boat drop me off
at a Japanese battlefield in Indonesia?
I was only 12.
My friend just 15.

There, at the battlefield
lines of dozens, hundreds of military men
battling to solve their sexual cravings.
You say I went there on my own two feet?
You say I decided to go there to be a sex slave
to those soldiers
facing war and miserable death day by day?

Was that a factory?

Ask your own daughter.
Ask your own 14 year old girl.

慰安婦 11

なんですって?
強制連行じゃなかったって言うんですか

工場に就職させてやるって言ったから付いていったのに
船から下ろされた所が
インドネシアの日本の戦場だったじゃないですか
私は12歳でした
私の友だちは15歳でした

じゃあ私が戦場の
男の軍人たちが数十名、数百名、列を作って
性的欲求を解消しようとする地獄の戦場に
自分の足で自分から行ったって言うんですか
戦場と残酷な死を随時経験する
軍人たちの
性奴隷として自分ですすんで行ったって言うんですか

そこが工場だったですか

あなたの娘に訊いてみて下さい
あなたの14歳の孫娘に訊いてみて下さい

위안부 12
— 강제연행 1

양산읍 시골 깡촌
아버지 돌아가시고 농사지을 남자가 없었어요

어느 날 동네 반장이 나에게,
공장에 일하러 가야 한다
안 가면 재산을 몰수하고 외국으로 추방시키겠다
고 협박했지요
시집가야 하는데 동네에 남자가 없었어요
남자는 모두 징용으로 끌려가버렸지요
제 나이 열네 살이었어요

끌려가서 스물한 살까지 노예로 살았어요
중국 광저우, 홍콩, 말레이시아, 인도네시아, 방콕, 싱가포르
끌려 다니는 데는 이유가 없었어요
그냥 트럭에 싣고 갈 뿐이었어요
제가 힘없는 농민의, 힘없고 어린 딸이라는 이유만으로.

생각해 보세요
열네 살이 잡혀가서 낯선 나라, 낯선 군인들에게
수십 명의 남자들에게 당하는 고통을 상상해보세요

그곳이 공장이라구요?
제가 열네 살인데

제가 스물한 살까지 팔년의 세월동안
군인의 노예로 살았는데
그곳을 공장이라고 믿으라고 하는 건가요?

Female Slave 12
   — Forced Haul 1

In our remote village in Yangsan county
Dad died and there were no men to work the farm

One day the village headman came to me
and said I had to go work in a factory
If I didn't go, he threatened
to seize our property and exile us from Korea
There were no men left in the village for me to marry
They had all been taken to be soldiers

This was when I was 14

Dragged away to work as a sex slave until I was 21
In Guangzhou, in Hong Kong, Malaysia, Bangkok, Singapore
They had no reason to take me
But they threw me in a truck and took me
I was just a helpless farm kid, a helpless young girl

Think about it.
Imagine suffering at the hands of dozens of men
in a strange country with strange soldiers, at only 14.

You say that was a factory?

I was 14.
For eight years until I was 21
I was a slave for the soldiers.
You expect me to believe that was a factory?

慰安婦 12
― 強制連行 1

梁山邑*の片田舎
父が亡くなってから農業を営む男がいませんでした

ある日、村の班長が私に
工場へ働きに出なければいけない
そうしなければ財産を没収して国外追放すると
脅迫しました
嫁に行かねばならないのに村には男がいませんでした
男はすべて徴用で引っ張られて行きました
私の年は14でした

連れて行かれて21歳まで奴隷生活をしました
中国の広州、香港、マレーシア、インドネシア、バンコック、シンガポール
引っ張られて行くのに理由はありませんでした
だた、トラックに乗せられて連れて行かれるだけでした
私が力のない農民の、力のない幼い娘だという理由だけで、

考えてみてください
14歳の子が捕まえられて連れて行かれ、見知らぬ国、見知らぬ軍人に
数十人の男たちにやられるのを想像してみてください

そこが工場だなんて言えますか
私が14歳から
21歳まで8年の歳月の間
軍人の奴隷として生活したのに
そこを工場だと信じろと言うのでしょうか

<訳者注>
* 梁山邑(ヤンサンウプ):韓国の慶尚南道に属する行政区画。

위안부 13
― 강제연행 2

어머니,
제가 살아 돌아왔어요
몇 번이고 죽으려고 시도했지만
몸만 상하고 돌아왔어요

어머니 보고 싶었어요
보고 싶어서 밤마다 울었어요

밤마다 악몽을 꾸고
몸을 부르르 떨었어요
지금도 악몽을 꾸고
괴로워요

제가 어떻게 잊을 수 있나요?
저도 잊고 싶어요
공포와 치욕과 고통을 잊고 싶어요

어머니,
제가 아직도 이렇게 고통스러운데
제가 군인들을 위안했다고
저들이 거짓말하네요.
어머니, 저들이 웃으며 거짓말하네요.

Female Slave 13
— Forced Haul 2

Mother,
I survived and I came back
Many times I tried to die
I came back with my whole body ruined

I wanted to see you, Mother
I cried every night because I wanted to see you

Every night I had nightmares
My body trembled in fear
Even now I have nightmares
It is agony

How can I forget?
I want to forget all about it
to forget the horror and the disgrace and the pain.

Mother,
It is still so hard for me
They say I comforted the soldiers.
They are lying.
Mother, they tell lies behind their smiles.

慰安婦 13
― 強制連行 2

お母さん
私、生きて帰ってきました
何度も死のうとしましたが
体だけが壊れて帰ってきました

お母さん、会いたかったです
会いたくて毎晩泣きました

夜ごとに悪夢を見て
体をぶるぶる震わせました
今でも悪夢を見るので
苦痛です

私がどうしたら忘れられるでしょうか
私も忘れたいです
恐怖と恥と苦痛を忘れたいです

お母さん、
私は今もこんなに苦しいのに
私が軍人たちを慰安したと
あの人たちは嘘をつきます
お母さん、あの人たちは笑いながら嘘をつきます

위안부 14
— 강제연행 3

내가 죽고 나면 역사가 묻히나?
역사는 살아서 꿈틀거릴 거야
뱀의 혀처럼 사실을 날름날름 기억시킬 거야

열세 살 소녀는
취직 시켜준다는 속임수에 넘어가,
가서 보니
만주 일본군 전쟁터였어
도망가려고 발버둥 쳤지만 불가능했어
일본군의 성노예생활을 했어
끔찍하고 무서웠어
죽으려고 했으나 몸만 망가졌어

일본으로부터 해방되던 날
나는 방에서 나오지 못했어
꽃처럼 아름다워야 할 열여덟 처녀

자궁이 망가져
이십대에 자궁을 적출했어

설움과 아픈 기억이
온몸을 넝쿨처럼 싸고 있어
치욕과 불행의 기억이

나를 칭칭 감고 망가진 시절로 나를 끌고 가.

내가 지금 팔십이 넘었어
꽃처럼 고운 나이에
망가진 몸
망가진 마음

글자로 하나하나 기록하여
그 죄과를 전해다오
고통과 슬픔으로 각인된 증거를
길이길이 전해다오.

Female Slave 14
— Forced Haul 3

If I die will this history be buried?
This history must live and must not keep still
darting quickly like a viper's tongue to make you remember

A girl of only 13
fooled by the promise of a job
Arriving there
it was the Japanese army's battlefield in Manchuria
I tried to kick and escape but it was impossible
I became a sex slave for the Japanese soldiers
So cruel and terrifying
I tried to kill myself, but instead just ruined my body

The day we were liberated from Japan
I could not come out of my room
An 18 year old girl who should be a beautiful flower

My womb was ruined
and in my 20s it was taken out

Memories of grief and pain
wrap around my body like vines
dragging me back, memories of disgrace and unhappiness

wrapped around and around my ruined body

Now I am more than 80
when I was a young beautiful flower
a ruined body
a ruined mind

Word by word it is all recorded
those sins will be told
The proof engraved by my suffering and sorrow
will tell the truth forever and ever

慰安婦 14
── 強制連行 3

私が死んだら歴史が埋められるだろうか
歴史は生きてうごめくだろう
蛇の舌のように、事実をペロペロと思い出させるだろう

13歳の少女は
就職させてやるという話に騙され、
行ってみたが
そこは満州の日本軍の戦場だった
逃げようともがいたけれど不可能だった
日本軍の性奴隷の生活をしたの
惨たらしくて恐ろしかった
死のうとしたけれど、体が壊れただけだった

日本から解放された日
私は部屋から出られなかった
花のように美しいはずの１８の生娘

子宮が壊れて
20代で子宮を摘出した

悲しみと苦痛の記憶が
全身を蔓のように包んでいる
恥辱と不幸の記憶が

私をぐるぐると巻いて、壊れた頃に私を引っ張って行く。

私は今、80を超えた
花のようにきれいなはずの年で
壊れた体
壊れた心

文字で一つ一つ記録して
その罪科を伝えておくれ
苦痛と悲しみで刻印された証拠を
永遠に伝えておくれ。

위안부 15
― 김달선

붉은 꽃잎이 떨어진다
자꾸 떨어진다
뇌리 속에 박힌 돌덩이가 꽃잎보다 더
붉은 피를 흘린다

한때는 뜨거운 입술들이 폭풍우 속 바다처럼
출렁거렸지만
이제 목소리는 잦아지고 옅어져간다

전장으로 끌려간 꽃들이 피멍 들고
곤죽이 되어 붉은 꽃잎만 떨어뜨렸다
생이 그때부터 해체되는 줄 알았다
열여덟 살 누이가 시들지 않는 목소리로
운다, 운다

흥해에서 어머니와 청어 팔다가
일본군에게 끌려간 열여덟 살 인간꽃
미얀마에서 위안부로 고초를 겪었다

지옥을 건너 밤을 건너
늙은 바닷가에 다시 왔다
무진장 멍든 꽃이
뼈를 깎는 비바람을 온몸으로 맞았다

계절은 멈출 줄 모르고
가는 숨결에도 멍들이 밤마다 통증을 되새겼다
폭염보다 더 날카로운 입술로 생의 진액을 흡수한
뼛속까지 탈진시킨 입들은 오늘도 거짓으로
하얗게 칠하고 있는 중이다
아무리 칠해도 겉만 칠할 뿐인 것을
속으로는 다 알면서!

눈물, 작별인사 따위로 용서 해주고 싶지 않다
지은 죄를 고통으로 감당해야지
넓은 태평양 한가운데서
외롭게.

Female Slave 15
― Kim Dal-seon

Crimson petals fall and fall again
But more than the petals
From the stones that stick in my memory
Crimson blood flows

Those hot lips once
Surged like the ocean in a raging storm
Now their voice fades and pales

A flower dragged to the battlefield and bruised
Naught remains but wilted falling crimson petals
Knowing then that life was finished
The voice of my 18 year old sister fades not
But cries and cries

After selling herring with Mother at Heunghae
An 18 year old flower, dragged away by the Japanese army
To suffer as a female slave in Myanmar

Going beyond hell, going beyond the night
Returning to the shore, now aged
A flower covered with bruises
Wind and rain whittle away her spirit

Maybe the seasons have stopped turning
Each night's passing breath
A bruise fixed in memory
The nectar of life absorbed
By lips sharper than scorching heat
Exhausted to the bones once again
By lips that to part to tell their lies
Trying to paint the paper white
Try and try again; only the surface changes
The truth inside cannot be hidden

Not wishing to grant any forgiveness with farewells or tears
The sins must be borne as suffering
In the middle of the vast Pacific
Desolate

慰安婦 15
　― 김달선(キム・ダルソン)

赤い花びらが散る
しきりに散る
脳裏に刻み込まれた石が花びらより多くの
赤い血を流す

一頃は熱い口唇が嵐の中の海のように
大きくうねったが
今、声は静まり 薄くなって行く

戦場に引かれて行った花々が深く傷ついて
めちゃくちゃになり、赤い花びらだけを散らした
生がそのときから解体されると思った
18の姉がしおれていない声で
泣く、泣く

興海*でお母さんとニシンを売りに行ったとき
日本軍に捕まえられて行った18歳の人の花
ミャンマーの慰安婦になって辛酸をなめた

地獄をわたり夜をわたり
古い海辺にまたやって来た
ものすごく傷ついた花が
骨までこたえる風雨に全身を晒した

季節はとどまることを知らず
かすかな息遣いにも傷口は毎晩痛みをほじくり返した
猛暑よりもっと鋭い唇で生の精を吸取り
骨の髄まで貪りつくした口は今日も偽りを
白く塗りたくっている
どんなに塗っても表を塗るだけだと
心はちゃんと分かっているくせに！

涙、さようならの言葉なんかで赦してやりたくない
犯した罪を苦痛で償うべきだ
広い太平洋の真ん中で
寂しく。

<訳者注>
* 興海(フンヘ)：韓国の慶尙北道浦にある町で、キム・ダルソンさんの故郷。

위안부 16
― 김연희

> 열두 살에 일본인 교장에게 차출돼
> 영문도 모른 채 일본으로 끌려가
> 시모노세키를 거쳐 도야마겡의 한 비행기 부속공장에서
> 9개월간 일하다가 아오모리겡 위안소에 끌려가
> 7개월간 위안부 생활을 했다.

백일홍 피같이 붉게 피었다
전장의 송곳으로 온몸에 찔려 한평생 낭자한 상처로
얼얼하게 살았다

너무 어렸다 너무 어려서 드센 인간파도가 두려웠다
무섭고 무서워, 무섭기만 했다
오장육부로 스미는 절규

환청이 잠을 흔들고 몸을 뒤집었다
잊고 싶었으나 잊히지 않는 지옥의 기억이
무섭고 두려웠다 밤이 두려웠다

고통에 체해서 몸이 아팠고
등허리에 숨은 치욕이 목숨을 갉아먹었다
살아갈 날들이 잘게 찢어져 널브러졌다
심하게 구부러진 시간은 펴지지 않고
엉켜 물러날 줄 몰랐다

전장에서 뭉개어진 십대를 돌려놓아라
늪을 만들고 내 만신창이 앞에서
뻔뻔하게도 너는 웃고 있다

사랑할 정신조차 탈색시켜버린 폭력을
너는 부인하고 있다

창문마다 내 순수한 열두 살의 마음을 걸어놓고
구름 속으로 들어가
울음을 울어댈 것이다
너는 내 곡소리를 외면하지 못하고

온몸으로 젖으며 들을 것이다.

Female Slave 16
— Kim Yeon-hee

Recruited at twelve by a Japanese headmaster
not even knowing the reason when taken to Japan
through Shimonoseki to an airplane parts factory in Toyama Prefecture;
then after working nine months dragged to Aomori to an Imperial Army brothel
to live as a female slave for seven months.

A Zinnia that bloomed blood-red
Her entire being pierced by the battlefield's auger
A lifetime turned to turmoil by burning wounds

Too young, too young, the wild human wave terrifying
Frightening, more frightening, nothing but frightening
Her piercing gut-wrenching scream

Sleep rent by delirium her body twists in torment
Trying to forget the memory of hell that cannot be forgotten
Frightening, terrifying, the night is now a terror

Body aching in overwhelming pain
With each deep breath the indignity whittles away at life
The passing days torn to small pieces and scattered
Time, all bent over, does not open up
Not realizing it is tangled and drifting away

Give back those teenage years trampled on the battlefield.
In front of my anguished wound-covered body
You shamelessly laugh

The violence that has sapped away even my will to love
You do not even acknowledge

My innocent 12-year old spirit dangling from every window
I retreat into the clouds
To cry unending tears
You cannot turn away from my wailing cries

Your whole body will be drenched as you listen

慰安婦 16
　　― 김연희(キム・ヨンヒ)

12歳のとき、日本人の校長に呼ばれて
わけも知らず日本に引かれて行き
下関を経て富山県のある飛行機の部品工場で
9ヵ月間働いてから青森県に引かれて行き
7ヵ月間慰安婦として生活した

ヒャクニチソウ、血のように赤く咲いた
戦場の錐で全身が突き刺され、一生そのおびただしい傷に
ヒリヒリさせられながら生きた

幼過ぎた、あまりにも幼かったので荒い人間の波が恐ろしかった
怖くて怖くて、ただただ怖かった
五臓六腑にしみわたる絶叫

幻聴が眠りを揺すって私の体はひっくり返える
忘れたかったけれど忘れられない地獄の記憶が
怖くて恐怖だった、夜が恐ろしかった

苦痛に胃がもたれて体調が悪く
背筋に隠れた恥辱が命をかじり取っていた
生きていくべき日々がばらばらに破れて散らかった
ひどく曲げられた時間は真っすぐにならず
もつれて退くことを知らなかった

戦場で踏みにじられた１０代を元に戻せ
沼を作って満身創痍になった私の前で
ずうずうしくもお前は笑っていた

愛する心まで脱色させてしまった暴力を
お前は認めないでいる

窓ごとに私の12歳の純粋な心をかけて
雲の中に入り込み
いつまでも泣こう
お前は私の慟哭する声を無視できずに
全身を濡らしながら聞くしかないのだ

위안부 17
— 환생

      이효순 처녀 열일곱 살에 의령 빨래터에서 일본군에 끌려가
    광복이 될 때까지 대만, 싱가폴, 베트남 등에서 위안부 생활 강요당함
  김외한金外漢 처녀 안동에서 열 한 살에 일본 홋가이도로 끌려가 위안부 고초

나는 라일락이었어
남산 다람쥐였어

나는 싱거운 달이었어
포항 숭어였어

갑자기 지구 밖으로 끌려간 처녀들
침묵으로 살 것
서로 감시할 것
고난이 아니고 성전의 전사들이라고 믿을 것
날마다 부서져서 핏물이 온몸을 적셔도
이건 성전이라고 믿을 것

뜨거운 바람보다 더 뜨거운 눈물이 쏟아져도
군화는 전쟁에 중독되어 눈물을 이해하지 못했다

어둠은 길었고 영혼은 저항의 불길을 지폈다
이 밤이 끝나면 빛나는 아침으로 다시 태어나리라

교활한 입들이 상처를 외면하고
역사를 지우개로 지우고 있다

찢긴 시간의 그림자가 길다
나는 불치의 아픔을 가졌어
무기력과 분노의 파도가 연달아 물결쳤어
기억을 분해시키려는 음모가 개떼처럼 덤볐어
나는 간절하게
집요하게 염원을 키웠어

밟혀서 납작해졌다가 다시
스멀스멀 끈질기게 살아나는 정신

너희들이 지은 죄 모습이 날마다 뚜렷해지리라
너희들이 지울수록 붉게 진해지리라

나는 이제 몸을 갈아타려고 하는 중이다
열여섯 꽃처녀로 탈바꿈하는 중이다

Female Slave 17
— Reincarnation

Hyosun Lee, a girl of 17 dragged away from Uiryeong as she laundered clothes at a washing place near a stream
Forced to be a female slave until Korea's liberation in Taiwan, Singapore, Vietnam and elsewhere
Kim Wehan, taken from Andong at eleven to suffer as a female slave in Hokkaido

I was a lilac
I was a squirrel at Namsan mountain

I was a whimsical moon
I was a silver mullet from Pohang

Innocent girls suddenly yanked off the earth
To live in silence
Watching over each other
Believing this is not suffering you are soldiers in a holy war
Broken open every day, and stained with blood
Believing this is a holy war

   Even though burning tears pour down, hotter than the hot wind
   The war-addicted combat boots could not understand the tears

   In the long darkness souls burned with a flame of resistance

Waiting for new life in the bright morning after the night

Artful lips turn away from the hurt
Rubbing out the past with an eraser

The torn shadow of time lengthens
Burdening me with incurable agony
Hit by continuous waves of helplessness and anger
The schemes to destroy my memories attacked as if by a pack of dogs
  Yet earnestly and
Stubbornly I clung to my desire

A spirit trampled on, snatched away, then once again
Uncannily, persistently brought back to life

Each day the image of your crimes more clear
The more you rub them out, the more scarlet the horror

I am going to move into a new body.
I am going to transform into an unstained girl of 16.

慰安婦 17
― 転生

　　　　이효순(イ・ヒョスン)は17歳の時、宜寧*の洗濯場から日本軍に引かれて行き
　　　　祖国の解放まで台湾、シンガポール、ベトナムなどで慰安婦生活を強いられた
　　　　金外漢(キム・ウェハン)は11歳の時、安東*から北海道に引かれて行き
　　　　　　　　　　　　　　　　　　　　　　　　　　　　慰安婦の辛酸をなめた

私はライラックだった
南山*のリスだった

私は淡い月だった
浦項*のボラだった

突然、地球の外へ引かれて行った娘たち
沈黙して生きること
互いに監視すること
苦難ではなく聖戦の戦士だと思うこと
毎日壊されて血が全身を濡らしても
これは聖戦だと信じること

熱い風よりもさらに熱い涙があふれ出ても
軍靴は戦争に中毒していてその涙を理解出来なかった

闇は長く魂は抵抗の火の手をあげた
この夜が終われば輝く朝に生まれ変わるだろう

狡猾な口が傷を無視して
歴史を消しゴムで消している

裂かれた時間の影が長い
私は不治の苦痛を身に持ってしまった
無気力と怒りの波が続けてしぶいた
記憶を分解させようとする陰謀が犬の群れのように飛び掛ってきた
私は切々と
執拗に念願を育てた

踏まれてぺっちゃんこにされても再び
もぞもぞと根気よく蘇る精神

お前たちの犯した罪が日に日に明確になるだろう
お前たちが無くそうとするほどさらに赤く濃くなるだろう

私は今、体を乗り替えている途中だ
16歳の花のような娘に衣替えの最中だ

<訳注>
*宜寧(ウィリョン)：韓国の慶尙南道にある郡で、イ・ヒョスンの故郷。
*安東(アンドン)：韓国の慶尙北道にある市で、キム・ウェハンの故郷。
*南山(ナムサン)：韓国の慶尙北道宜寧にある山。
*浦項(ポハン)：韓国の慶尙北道にある市。

고마워요

고마워요
끔찍한 전쟁에서
더 끔찍한 고통을 당하신 할머니께서
노예의 삶을 숨기지 않으시고
세상에 알려주셔서 고마워요

용기 있게 사실을 말해주셔서 감사해요
부끄러움 때문에 힘드셨을 텐데
당당히 밝혀주셔서 감사해요

할머니께서 침묵하셨다면
어린 제가 할머니의 고통을
어찌 알 수 있었을까요

일본은 있었던 사실조차
부인하고 있잖아요?

몇몇은 개인의 이익 때문에
입을 다물고 있겠지요

할머니 힘내세요
제가 할머니의
든든한 손길이 되어드릴게요

저는 할머니가 자랑스러워요

Thank You

Thank you
In that terrible war
Such a brave old woman, you endured even more terrible suffering
for not hiding your life as a slave
Thank you for telling the world

Thank you for telling the truth with courage
so difficult because of the shame
Thank you for telling everything clearly

Brave woman, if you had kept silent
would I have had the chance in my youth
to know how you had suffered?

Doesn't Japan deny
that it even happened?

For the benefit of a few people
you could have kept your silence

You brave old woman, take heart
I will stand here
strong beside you

I am so proud of you, you brave lady

ありがとうございます

ありがとうございます
惨い戦争で
さらに惨い苦痛を受けたおばあさんが
奴隷だった生活を包み隠さずに
世の中に知らせてくださってありがとうございます

勇気を出して事実を言ってくださって感謝します
恥かしさのために辛かったはずなのに
堂々と明かしてくださって感謝します

おばあさんが黙っていたなら
若い私がおばあさんの苦痛を
理解できたはずがありません

日本は存在した事実さえ
否定しているでしょう?

何人かは個人の利益のために
口を閉ざしているのでしょう

おばあさん、頑張ってください
私がおばあさんの
心強い味方になりますから

私はおばあさんが誇らしいです

증언 1

나는 어쩌다 여기에 잡혀왔나
시간이 멈추면 이 고통도 멈출까

허공을 뚫고 떨어지는 빗방울
억수같이 내려서 내가 떠내려 가버렸으면!
지옥 같은 위안소 떠내려 가버렸으면!

내 맨몸을 짓밟고
맨 정신을 짓누르고
망치로 머리를 치는 듯
나는 몇 번이나 혼절했던가

어혈과 피곤으로 온몸이 지치고
혈관마다 폐수 흐르는 듯

어둠과 울음이 전신을 흘러
사방이 막막하여 가슴이 미어지고

몸은 끝없이 추락하고
정신은 가물거리다가 솟구치곤 했어

감시는 무시무시했어
녹초가 된 몸이 견고한 감시망을 빠져나가지 못했어

공포에 짓눌려 신음도 삼켰어
까무러치면 살려내서 내 몸을 착취했어

무서워 벌벌 떨었어
숨 막히는 공포와 고통에 온몸이 피폐해갔어

강철 같은 정신으로 견뎠어
잔인한 시간을 버텼어

Witness 1

Somehow I was captured and brought here
If time stops will this pain stop too?

Falling raindrops pierce the empty space
if I had just been swept away by the downpour!
I could have escaped from this hell of an army brothel!

My naked body trampled
my naked spirit oppressed
like a hammer pounded my head
or I fainted over and over

My whole body wearied with bruises and fatigue
as if every blood vessel flowed with waste water

Darkness and sorrow streamed from my whole body
loneliness from all directions tore at my chest

My body plummeting without end
my spirit flickered and blazed

Terrified by the guards
my utterly spent body could not escape their iron net

My moans swallowed up by oppressive fear
when I passed out my body revived so they exploited it

Trembling with fear
breath-stopping terror and pain have exhausted my whole being

Bearing it all with a spirit like steel
I held on all through that brutal time

証言 1

私は一体どうしてここに捕まって来たのか
時間が止まればこの苦しみも止まるだろうか

虚空を突き破って落ちる雨のしずく
土砂降りになって私を押し流してしまったらいい！
地獄のような慰安所、押し流してしまったらいい！

私の体は踏みにじられ
精神は押さえつけられ
金づちで頭を打たれるように
私は何度昏絶したことか

皮下出血と疲労のせいで全身が弱り
血管はすべて廃水が流れるよう

暗闇と慟哭が全身を流れて
四方が真っ暗で胸が張り裂け

体は果てしなく墜落してゆき
精神は朦朧としたり煮えたぎったりした

監視はものすごかった
へとへとの体は強固な監視網から抜け出すことはできなかった

恐怖に打ちひしがれて呻き声さえも呑み込んだ
気が遠くなれば生き返らせて私の体を搾取した

怖くてぶるぶる震えた
息詰まる恐怖と苦痛で全身が疲弊して行った

鋼鉄のような精神で耐え抜いた
残酷な時間を持ち堪えた

증언 2

일본군은 나를 막사에 밀폐시켰어
위안소에 붙은 물건처럼

나는 슬픔중독자가 되어
밤마다 꿈속마다 어머니를 찾아 헤맸어

고향은 너무 멀었고
어머니도 너무 멀리 있었어

아프고 슬픈 나는
내 몸을 파먹는 군인 때문에
온몸이 고통으로 울부짖었어

위안소 구석에 구겨져
벌레처럼 웅크리고
울었어

얼음장 같은 분노는
스멀스멀 커갔어

녹지 않고 차갑게 살아있어

만행들이

눈동자마다 똑똑히 각인되고
온몸에 새겨져 기록되었어

찬란한 햇빛에
역사적 기록이 노출되기 시작했어

Witness 2

Locked up in the barracks by the Japanese Army
treated just like army brothel property

Consumed with sadness I wandered
every night in my dreams searching for my mother

Home was too far away
Mother was also too far away

In pain and sadness
because of the soldiers who ate into my body
my whole being screamed in pain

In the corner of the brothel
huddled just like a bug
I sobbed

Resentment crept and grew
like a slab of ice

Frozen, I lived without melting

Their atrocities

recorded clearly in the pupil of each eye
the record carved on my whole body

The brilliant sunlight
has started to expose the record of my history

証言 2

日本軍は私を兵舎に閉じ込めた
慰安所に付いた品物のように

私は悲しみの中毒者になって
夜ごと夢ごとに母をさがし回った

故郷はあまりに遠く
母もあまりに遠くにいた

苦痛で悲しい私は
自分の体を貪る軍人のせいで
全身の苦しみで泣き叫んでいた

慰安所の隅に縮こまって
虫のようにしゃがんで
泣いた

凍てつくような怒りは
もぞもぞと大きくなった

溶けずに冷たく生きている

蛮行が

二つの瞳にまざまざと焼き付けられ
全身に刻まれて記録された

燦爛たる日差しに
歴史的な記録がさらされ始めた

증언 3

아침마다 눈을 뜨면
신음과 피멍의 처참한 시간이 이어졌습니다

투명한 유리 상자에 갇힌 벌레처럼
온몸으로 부딪치며 살갗이 찢어지고
다리가 부러지도록 벗어나려고 애썼습니다

절망과 슬픔으로 출렁이다가
차라리 내가 의자가 되고 침대가 되어
삐걱거리고 부서지고 싶었습니다

나는 전쟁터에 유폐되어
고향은 나를 잃어버렸습니다
뼈마디가 쑤시고 가슴이 저려 와도
열네 살 소녀는 눈에 피가 맺히도록 울어도
구원받지 못하였습니다

열대의 물렁한 태양이 늘어지게 뜨거워도
시원한 소식이 없었습니다
버티며 기다리다가
나는 차라리 핏물로 환생하는 꽃이 될 지경이었습니다

공장에서 돈 벌게 해주겠다는 유인에 속아

함께 가지 않으면 집안을 망하게 해버리겠다는 협박이 무서워
당신을 따라나선 나는 유괴된 소녀였습니다
전쟁터 위안소가 공장이라구요?

불타오르는 분노와 시퍼런 슬픔이 정신을 찢고
몸은 만신창이로 생의 바닥으로 가라앉았습니다

피멍으로 얼룩진 몸이 병들고
정신은 찢어져 아직도 밤마다 악몽을 꿉니다

세월이 흘렀다고요?
세월이 흘러서 당신은 잊었나 봅니다
제 신경 마디마디에
고통의 역사가 기록되어 있습니다

저도 한 송이 꽃으로 곱게 피었더랬습니다
무참히 짓밟힌 나의 청춘에게 당연히
당신은 사과해야 하지 않겠습니까?

Witness 3

Every morning when I opened my eyes
I was still there in the misery of groans and bruises

Like a bug confined in a glass box
I bumped against the walls and my skin was torn
I tried to climb out until my legs were broken

After waves of longing and sadness
I wished I could just be a chair or a bed
That I could just shout out and break in pieces

I was confined on the battlefield
forgotten by my hometown
my joints aching and my chest numb
a girl of 14 crying until her eyes are red
with no chance to be rescued

As the abundant rays of the tropical sun grew hot
there was no refreshing news
If I could just hold on and wait
through that blood I could be reborn as a flower

Deceived to think I could make money in a factory

terrified that if I did not go my family would suffer
By following you I became a girl in bondage
You say this battlefield brothel is a factory?

Burning anger and powerful sorrow tear my spirit
my life at rock bottom, my body all spent

Discolored with bruises my body falls ill
my spirit torn, I still have nightmares every night

You say time has gone by?
I guess you forgot as time went by
But my every nerve
holds the memory of that history of pain

They said I bloomed as a beautiful flower
Don't you have to apologize for cruelly
trampling the bloom of my youth?

証言3

毎朝目を開ければ
呻き声と苦痛の凄惨な時間が続きました

透明なガラスの箱に閉じ込められた虫のように
全身でぶつかって肌が裂け
足が折れるほど抜け出そうと努力しました

絶望と悲しみで波打っては
いっそ私が椅子やベットになって
軋んで壊れたいと思いました

私は戦場に幽閉され
故郷は私を失ってしまいました
骨節がうずいて胸が痛んでも
14歳の少女は目に血が滲むほど泣いても
救われませんでした

熱帯の柔らかい太陽がぐったりするほど暑くても
気持ちの良い便りはありませんでした
堪えて待ちながら
私はいっそ血で生まれ変わる花になるところでした

工場で稼げるようにしてやるという誘引に騙され

一緒に行かなければ家をつぶしてやるという脅迫が怖くて
あなたについて行った私は、誘拐された少女でした
戦場の慰安所が工場だなんて

沸き上がる怒りや蒼白の悲しみが精神を引き裂き
体は満身創痍になって生のどん底に沈みました

青黒いあざだらけになった体は病み
精神は裂かれて未だに夜ごと悪夢を見ます

歳月が流れただろうって?
歳月が流れてあなたは忘れたようですね
私の神経の節々に
苦しみの歴史が記録されています

私も一輪の花として美しく咲いていたのでした
無惨に踏みにじられた私の青春に当然
あなたは謝罪すべきではないでしょうか。

기도

신이여
이 어둠의 세계를 벗어나게 해 주십시오
저 푸른 하늘 날아서
고향으로 가게 해 주십시오

고통으로 타오르는 몸을 식혀주시고
슬픔으로 꺼져가는 몸을 건져 주십시오

연약한 살결이 터져서
정신이 자주 어둠 속으로 빠져 들어갑니다

가슴이 갈라지고
억장이 무너지는 시간이 이어집니다

제 몸과 정신을
끝없는 폭력에서 구해주시고
바스러져가는 정신을
깨어있게 해 주십시오

전신에 피멍이 들어도
상처투성이로 얼룩 져도
살아있게 힘을 주십시오

살아서 증언하게 해 주십시오
지금의 모든 신음을 언어로
세상에 알리도록
견디는 힘을 주십시오

앙상한 뼈로 남더라고
증언할 힘을 주십시오

망각의 땅에 가더라도 잊지 않고
증언하는 입술을 주십시오

Prayer

O Father in heaven
please deliver me from this world of darkness
Let me fly through the blue skies
and go back home

Please cool the blazing pain in my body
rescue my body vanishing in sorrow

My delicate being burst open
my spirit descends into darkness

My breast torn apart
soon I will collapse entirely

Please rescue my body and spirit
from this endless violence
Please reawaken
my crumbling spirit

Even though my body is covered with bruises
even though I am spotted with wounds
give me the strength to keep living

Let me live so I can be a witness
Let all my moans become words
to let the world know
Give me the strength to endure

Even if I am only skin and bones
give me the strength to testify

Though I go to a forgotten land help me recall and
give me the lips to testify

祈り

神よ
この暗闇の世界から抜け出させてください
あの青い空を飛んで
故郷に行かせてください

苦しみで燃え立つ体を冷まし
悲しみで消え入る体をお救いください

か弱い肌が裂けて
精神がしきりに闇の中に落ちて行きます

胸が張り裂け
そしてつぶれる時間が続きます

私の体と精神を
果てしなき暴力からお救いくださり
砕けていく精神を
眠らないように守ってください

全身に深い傷がついても
傷だらけになっても
生きているように力をください

生き残って証言させてください
今のすべての呻きを言葉で
世の中に知らせられるよう
耐えることのできる力をください

骨と皮ばかりになっていても
証言できる力をください

忘却の地に行ったとして忘れずに
証言できる唇をください

편지

어머니
새들은 하늘을 자유로이 날아가는데
저에게는 자유가 없습니다

구름은 자유로이 움직이며 고향으로 가는데
저는 잡혀 있습니다

어머니
구름은 슬프면 온몸으로 펑펑 울 수 있는데
저는 숨죽여 웁니다

제가 구름이라면 얼마나 좋을까요
먹장구름이 분노처럼 치밀어 솟아나면
실컷 쏟아지면 후련하겠지요

천둥치고 번개로 번득이며
치욕과 악몽과 온갖 설움과
견딜 수 없는 공포감을
발악하며 쏟아낼 수 있겠지요

인간을 짓밟으며 존엄성을 해치는
무리들에게 천둥치며 벌할 수 있겠지요

아, 제가 구름이라면 얼마나 좋을까요
하늘을 헤매다가 고향에 닿으면
어머니 앞에 쏟아지며 실컷 울 수 있을텐데요

어머니 저에게도 날개가 있다면
얼마나 좋을까요?
날아가 이 모든 고통과 슬픔을 말할 수 있을텐데요

새라면 날아가서 어머니 품에
살포시 내려 쉴 수 있을텐데요
따스하고 포근한 어머니 곁에서
잠들 수 있으면 얼마나 좋을까요

Letter

Mother
the birds fly freely in the sky
but I have no freedom

The clouds move freely towards our home
but I have been caught

Mother
If the clouds are sad they can cry with their all
but I must hide my sobs

How I wish I were a cloud
When black clouds surge and gush with anger
they can spew and flow as much as they want

As the lightning flashes and the thunder booms
I want desperately to let the shame
and the nightmares and the overwhelming sadness
and the terror that I cannot endure pour out of me

I want to send thunder and punishment to those gangs
who violate people's human dignity

O, how I wish I were a cloud
If I could wander through the sky and get back home
with you Mother I could pour out my heart and cry my fill

Mother if I had wings too
wouldn't that be wonderful?
I could fly away and end all of this pain and sorrow.

If I were a bird I could fly right to your arms, Mother
I could gently descend and rest there
If I could sleep there warm and soft at your side
how wonderful that would be

手紙

お母さん
鳥たちは空を自由に飛んで行くのに
私には自由がありません

雲は自由に動いて故郷へ向かうのに
私は捕まえられています

お母さん
雲は悲しければ全身でわあわあと泣けるのに
私は息を殺して忍び泣きます

私が雲だったらどんなにいいだろうって思います
黒い雲が怒りのように湧き上がって行くときには
思い切り降ったらすっきりするでしょう

雷が鳴って、稲妻が走れば
恥辱と悪夢とありとあらゆる悲しみと
堪えられない恐怖感を
あがきながら溢れさせるでしょう

人を踏みにじって尊厳性を傷つける
連中に雷を落として罰を与えられるでしょう

ああ！私が雲だったらどんなにいいだろうって思います
空を彷徨って故郷に着けば
お母さんの前で溢れるように思い存分泣けるでしょう

お母さん、私にも羽があったら
どんなにいいだろうって思います
飛んで行ってこの全ての苦痛や悲しみを言えるからです

鳥ならば飛んで行ってお母さんの懐に
そっと降りて休めるでしょう
温かくて柔らかいお母さんの側で
眠れるならどんなにいいだろうって思います

위안소 여자의 독백

열대의 밤
숨 막히는 고통이 복부를 뚫고 척추를 뚫어
맑고 투명한 정신을 으깨고
나를 씹어 먹는 허탈과
오그라들게 하는 감시로
내 몸은 찌그러들고 노래져 갔어

나의 밤은 눈물로 얼룩진
검은 강물로 흘렀어
뼛속까지 여위어 무력감에 찌든 몸
잔인한 폭력의 시간을 견디는 일
안식과 사랑은 꿈조차 꾸지 못했어

달빛도 시름으로 기침하는 밤
나는 껍질만 남아서
몸이 부서지듯 자주 아팠어
너무 아파 비린 나를
어둠조차 삼키지 못해서
아침마다 토해냈어

뜨겁고 끈적이는 아침의 아가리
무서웠어

Soliloquy of a Female Slave

On those nights in the tropics

Unbearable pain wracked my belly and my back
My clear bright spirit crushed
Kept under guard by the exhaustion and
withering that ate away at my very being
at my injured and jaundiced body

My nights were a tear-stained
river flowing with black water
My helpless form emaciated to the bone
While bearing that brutal violence
I could not even dream of rest or of love

Even the moonlight was disturbed by my woes
Nothing left of me but a shell
My body in agony as if ripped apart
The pain made me so loathsome
even the dark could not swallow me up
Coughed up again every morning

The sharp tongue of the hot sticky morning
So frightening

慰安所の女の独白

熱帯の夜
息詰まるほどの苦しみが腹を突き、脊椎を突いて
清らかで透明な精神を潰し
私を噛んで食べる虚脱感と
私を縮込ませる監視で
私の体は凹み、黄ばんでいく

私の夜は涙で染みのできた
黒い川のほうへと流れた
骨の髄まで痩せて無力感に染まった体
残酷な暴力の時間を耐えること
安息と愛は夢にも見ることができなかった

月明かりも憂いで咳をする夜
私は皮だけが残り
壊れたようにいつも体が痛かった
あまりの痛さで臭くなった私を
闇さえも呑み込めず
毎朝吐き出した

熱くてべたべたの朝の口
恐ろしかった

천개의 눈물

달빛이 어룽거리며
심장을 도려내는 서러움을 훑는다
사랑스런 소녀여
네 상처와 눈물을 닦아주리라

굽실거리지 않는 꼿꼿한 정신이
아프다
안간힘으로 버티어야지
정신마저 먹히지 말고 살아남아야지
살아남아 증언해야지

 도망치지 못하는 나는 죄인처럼 잡혀서
달빛 속에서 중얼거린다

피가 맺히는 밤
눈물도 숨결이 있어서
고통 속에서 가시 돋친 향기가 난다

아, 어긋나버린 내 삶의 물줄기여
달을 적시고 바람을 적시고
천지의 눈동자를 모두 적셔서
강철 마음을 녹이고 녹여서
마음마다 물길을 트게 해 다오

부서진 몸이 일어설 수 있도록
찢겨진 마음에 살점이 붙을 수 있도록
삶을 뜨겁게 껴안을 수 있도록
흐르고 소용돌이쳐 다오

천개의 눈물이여
살이 떨리는 두려움마저 쓸어가 다오

A Thousand Tears

The speckled moonlight
Licks at my grief-torn heart
Beloved sweet girl
Let me wipe your wounds and tears

Unyielding spirit that will not grovel
It hurts
Need to hang on with all my strength
Can't let my spirit be devoured, I must live
I must live so I can bear witness

Caught like a criminal I cannot escape
I mutter in the moonlight

Night, and my heart bleeds
The touch of my tears lingers
Amidst the pain a sharp scent arises

O, the course of my life that has gone astray
Has drenched the moon and the wind
Every eye in heaven and earth is wet
Melting and melting the iron-willed hearts
Every heart breaks open

So that my broken body can stand up
So that my ragged heart can have strength
So that my life can be warmly embraced
Let me flow and swirl

Let these thousand tears
Soothe the fear that makes my flesh tremble

一千粒の涙

月明かりがちらつき
心臓をえぐりとる悲しみを舐める
いとしい少女よ
お前の傷と涙を拭いてあげよう

へいこらしない剛直な精神が
痛い
あらん限りの力で耐えねば
精神だけは奪われずに生き残らねば
生き残って証言せねば

逃れられない私は罪人のように捕われて
月明かりの中で呟く

血のにじむ夜
涙にも息遣いがあり
苦痛の中で刺の立つ香りがする

ああ！食い違ってしまった私の生の水流よ
月を濡らし、風を濡らし
天地の瞳を全て濡らし
鋼鉄の心を溶かしては溶かし
すべての心に水路を開いておくれ

壊れた体が立ち上がれるように
張り裂けた心に肉がつくように
生を熱く抱きしめられるように
流れて渦巻いておくれ

一千粒の涙よ
肌身の震える恐怖まで掃いて行っておくれ

증언 4

방직공장에 취직시켜줄게
월급이 많아서 재봉틀도 살 수 있어

열네 살 소녀는 순진해서
일본인을 따라 배를 타고 히로시마로 갔어
벚꽃 만발한 히로시마 봄은 아름다웠어
더 어여쁜 시골 소녀는
돈 번다는 희망에 따라 갔어

배에서 내린 곳이 라바울 일본군위안소였어
온몸으로 반항했으나 죽도록 맞았어
감시는 엄했고 자유는 없었어
낮이고 밤이고 군인들이 수십 명 줄을 서곤 했어
괴롭고 아픈 노예 도망칠 수 없는 노예

폭격이 심해지자 동굴 안에 대피시켰어
정글 속으로 도망쳤어

전쟁이 끝나도 집에 가지 못했어
병이 너무 심했어
도시에서 돈 벌어 치료했어
나는 죽어도 일본정부의 사과를 받아야겠어
한창 고운 나이에 피멍들고 병든 내 몸,
황폐해진 내 정신을 배상받아야겠어.

Witness 4

Promised a job in a textile mill
And even the money for a sewing machine

This pure-hearted girl of 14
Took the boat to Hiroshima with the Japanese man
Hiroshima was beautiful with its spring cherry blossoms
And I an even more beautiful country girl
Following with the hope of earning money

Let off the boat at a Japanese army brothel in Rabaul
I resisted with all my strength but they beat me severely
The strict guards gave me no freedom
Day and night lines of soldiers waiting their turn with me
A slave in agony and pain, a slave with no way to escape

When the bombing got heavy they hid me in a cave
and I ran away into the jungle

The war ended, but I could not go home
I was too sick
Worked in the city to pay the doctors
I must get an apology from Japan or die trying
My body so bruised and sick at the peak of my youth
They must pay me for crippling my spirit.

証言 4

紡織工場へ就職させてやる
給料が高いからミシンも買えるぞ

14歳の少女はいとけなくて
日本人について行って船に乗り、広島へ渡った
桜の真っ盛りだった広島の春は美しかった
それよりきれいな田舎の少女は
お金を稼げるという希望を持って付いて行った

船から降りた所はラバウル*の日本軍慰安所だった
必死で反抗したけれど死ぬほど殴られた
監視は厳しく、自由は無かった
夜となく昼となく数十人の軍人たちが列を作った
辛くて苦痛の奴隷、逃げられない奴隷

爆撃が激しくなると洞窟の中へ待避した
ジャングルの中へ逃げた

戦争が終わっても家には戻れなかった
病気がひどかった
都市でお金を稼いで治療した
私は死んでも日本政府から謝罪の言葉を聞かねばならない
一番きれいな年に傷だらけになって病にかかった私の体

荒廃した私の精神を賠償してもらわなければ

<訳注>
*ラバウル：太平洋のニューブリテン島にある都市。第二次世界大戦(1939~1945)の時に日本の海軍航空隊などの基地があったところ。

봄 처녀

언니와 쑥 캐다가
일본경찰차에 납치되었다네

차를 타고 배를 타고
끌려가고 끌려가도 아무도 몰랐다네

그 놈의 쑥을 캐지 말았어야 했나
그 놈의 봄이 오지 말았어야 했나

오사카에서 학대를 받았네
너무나 고통스러워 정신이 혼미해져버렸네
군인들이 산속에 나를 버렸다네
나는 병원에 갇혔다네
고통의 환각과 망상에 갇혔다네
내 정신을 잃어버렸어
말도 잃어버렸어

고향땅에도 갈 수 없다네

Spring Maiden

While gathering mugwort with my sister
Seized and taken in a Japanese police car

They took me by car, then took me by ship
dragged around and dragged around and nobody knew

Should we have stayed out of that mugwort field
Would it have been better if spring hadn't come

Ill-treated in Osaka
it was so difficult my mind was confused
The soldiers abandoned me in the mountains
I was locked up in the hospital
Trapped by illusions and fantasies from the pain
I lost my mind
I lost my voice

I cannot even go back home

春の娘

お姉さんとヨモギを摘んでいるときに
日本のパトカーに拉致されたのさ

車に乗ったり、船に乗ったり
引かれて行っても引かれて行っても誰も知らなかったんだ

そのヨモギを摘みに行かなければよかったのか
その春が来なければよかったのか

大阪で虐待されたのさ
あまりに苦痛で精神が混迷に陥ってしまったんだ
兵士たちは山の中に私を捨てた
私は病院に閉じ込められた
苦痛の幻覚と妄想に閉じ込められたのさ
私は自分の精神を失ってしまったんだ
言葉も失ってしまった

故郷にも行けなくなったのさ

팔라우 섬 한인 소녀

환상의 섬 팔라우에서
지옥을 겪었습니다

고향에서 강제로 연행되어
멀리 참으로 멀리
남태평양 섬 팔라우
일본군 위안소에서
비참하게 노예로 살았습니다.

어느 임신한 위안부의 등에
폭탄을 장착시켜,
죽어가는 처녀의 절규가
포탄 연기 따라 메아리쳐서
듣는 이의 가슴이 찢겨져나갔습니다

폭격이 심해지자 위안부로 학대당해 병든
처녀들을 흙구덩이에 파묻었습니다
증거인멸
잔인한 증거인멸이 성공할 줄 알았겠지요

시간이 흘러서
흙에 파묻혔던 여자들이 사진첩에서
하나씩 살아나 몸을 일으켰어요

살아나서 역사상 가장 잔인했던
소녀 학대를 증언하기 시작했어요

진실을 잠시 몇 년 또는 몇 십 년 가릴 수는 있겠지요
하지만 영원히 가릴 수 없는 게 진실의 얼굴인 거죠
진실은 저 홀로 생명력이 있어서
거짓의 덮개가 얇아지면
툭 발을 내밀고
거짓의 막을 헤치고 튀어 나오죠

거짓이 부인할수록 진실의 힘이 거세어지고
물길이 되어 넘치게 되죠
진실은 없어지지 않는 힘을 천성적으로 가졌기 때문이죠

Korean Girls on the Islands of Palau

On the fantasy islands of Palau
We went through hell

Forced to leave our hometowns
far away, very far away
In the south Pacific islands of Palau
at a Japanese army brothel
We lived as miserable slaves

A bomb landed right on
one pregnant girl's back
The dying girl's screams
echoed through the smoke from the shelling
tearing at everyone who heard

When the bombing got heavier the female slaves, sick from the ill treatment
Were buried in holes in the ground
To destroy the evidence
Convinced their cold hearted destruction of evidence would succeed

As time went by

The girls buried in the ground were brought to life
standing in a photo album
Most heartlessly ill treated girls in history
brought to life to witness to the truth

The truth can be hidden for a few years, maybe a few decades
But the face of truth cannot be hidden forever
The truth is its own force of life
When the cover of falsehood becomes shallow
The truth can kick out at it
exposing the lies, and it will rush out

As the falsehood is denied, the truth grows more powerful
pouring out like a flooding stream
Because the truth has the power never to disappear

パラオ島の韓国人少女

幻想の島パラオで
地獄を経験しました

故郷から強制連行されて
遠く、あまりにも遠く
南太平洋の島パラオ
その日本軍慰安所で
悲惨な奴隷として生きていました

ある妊娠した慰安婦の背中に
爆弾を装着し、
死んでいく少女の絶叫が
砲弾の煙と共にこだまして
聞く者の胸が張り裂けていきました

爆撃が激しくなると、慰安婦として虐待されて病気になった
娘たちを土の穴に埋めました
証拠隠滅
残酷な証拠隠滅が成功するとでも思ったのでしょう

時間が経って
土に埋められた女たちが写真帖から
一人ずつ蘇って体を起こしました

生き返って歴史の中で最も残酷だった
少女虐待を証言し始めました

真実をしばし数年、または数十年覆い隠すことはできるでしょう
しかし永遠に覆い隠せないのが、真実の顔なのでしょう
真実はそれだけで生命力があるので
偽りの蓋が薄くなれば
足を突き出し
偽りの膜をかき分けて飛び出すでしょう

偽りが否定すればするほど真実の力はより強くなり
水路となって溢れるでしょう
真実は消えない力を天性として持っているためでしょう

콰이강의 다리

한때 태국 콰이강의 다리 옆에는
일본군 위안소가 있었지요

전쟁이 끝난 뒤 연합군 자료에 기록된
태국 포로수용소의 한인 위안부는
숫자로 천 5백여 명으로 표기되어 있었습니다

KBS 탐사보도팀이 최근 비밀 해제된
태국 군부 문서에서 이들의 명부를 발굴했습니다.
태국어와 영어로 작성된 2개의 명부에는
모두 463명의 이름이 적혀 있습니다.
1945년 10월부터 이듬해 4월까지,
태국 아유타야 수용소에 수감된 위안부들 입니다.
위안부가 아닌 간호조무사로 기록돼 있는데,
종전終戰 무렵 일본 해군 사령부는
간호조무사로 변경 등록하라는 비밀지령을 보냅니다

위안부의 존재를 감추기 위해서
증거인멸을 위해서

증거인멸하는 행위는 일본군이 위안부를
반인륜적으로 학대하고 유린하고 노예로 삼은 것을
인정하는 것이지요

진실은 억눌려 있다가 곳곳에서 꿈틀대며 살아나서
실체를 드러내어
눈이 어두웠던 이들의 눈을 뜨게 해주지요

콰이강 옆 진실이 은폐되었던 자리가 이제
노출되어 목소리들이 폭포처럼 쏟아지고 있지요

The Kwai River Bridge

At one time next to the Kwai River Bridge in Thailand
There was a Japanese army brothel

After the war on the lists the UN found
the names of the Korean female slaves in the POW camps
More than 1,500 were recorded there

The latest secret revealed by the KBS investigative reporters
was a list of them in Thai military documents
Two registers of names in Thai and English
a record of 463 names
From October 1945 until the next April
 women detained at the Autau concentration camp in Thailand.
 Listed not as female slaves, but nursing assistants
 At the war's end, the commanding Japanese naval officer
  ordered them to change the records and call them nursing assistants

To hide the existence of the female slaves,
To make the evidence disappear

The act of destroying evidence by the Japanese army

to hide the inhumane treatment of these ravaged and enslaved women
  confirms the truth of what they did

After the truth has been suppressed it twists and turns and comes to life
  exposing reality
  Opening the eyes of those whose vision had been dulled

Now the truth that was hidden next to the Kwai River
is exposed and its voices are pouring out like a cascade

クウェー川の橋

一時期、タイのクウェー川の橋の袂には
日本軍の慰安所がありました

戦争が終わった後に、連合軍の資料に記録された
タイの捕虜収容所の韓国人慰安婦は
数が1,500人余りと表記されていました

KBS放送探査報道チームは最近秘密解除された
タイ軍部文書から、この人たちの名簿を発見しました。
タイ語と英語で書かれた二つの名簿には
全部で463人の名前が書かれています。
1945年10月から翌年4月まで、
タイのアユタヤ収容所に収監された慰安婦たちです。
慰安婦ではなく、看護助手として記録されていますが、
終戦の頃、日本海軍司令部は
看護助手に変更して登録するように秘密指令を送ります。

慰安婦の存在を隠すために
証拠隠滅のために

証拠隠滅する行為は、日本軍が慰安婦を
反人倫的に虐待し、蹂躙し、奴隷にしたことを
認めることです

真実は抑えられていたが、あちこちで蠢いて生き返り
実体をさらけ出し
目の眩んだ人たちの目を開いてくれます

クウェー川の袂の真実が隠蔽されていた所が今
明らかになって「その声」が滝のように溢れています

아, 라멍 라멍
― 증거인멸

격전지 윈난성 서부 지역
한인 위안부 2백여 명
일본군이 패전했을 때
많은 위안부들이 살해됐고 동네 우물 곳곳에 버려졌다

아가야, 이 우물은 너무 차가워서
네 몸을 더 차갑게 하겠구나
네 절규가 핏빛으로 우물을 물들이고
천지를 물들이는구나

짓밟힌 몸이 부었구나
퉁퉁 부어
물이 너를 안고 붉게 통곡하는구나

라멍 사람들이 우는구나
물보다 귀한 아가들이 퉁퉁 부어
온몸으로 절규하는 소리에
가슴 찢어졌구나

Ah, Ramung, Ramung
— Vanishing Proof

In western Yunnan Province the site of a fierce battle
more than 200 female slaves from Korea
When the Japanese army was defeated
many of the women were killed and thrown in nearby wells

Sweet daughter, this well is too cold
Your body will get even colder
Your screams will paint this well red
They are painting all of heaven and earth red

Your trampled bodies are bloated
All fat and bloated
The water embraces you and it laments

The people of Ramung are crying
The girls more precious than water fat and bloated
The sound of them screaming with their whole bodies
Has torn their hearts to shreds

ああ!ラモウ、ラモウ*
― 証拠隠滅

激戦地だった雲南省の西部地域
韓国人慰安婦が200人余り
日本軍が敗戦した時
多くの慰安婦たちが殺され、近所のあちらこちらの井戸に捨てられた

娘よ、あの井戸はとても冷たくて
お前の体をもっと冷たくするだろう
お前の絶叫が血の色に井戸を染め
天地を染めるのだ

踏みにじられた体が膨れている
ぶくぶく膨れて
水がお前を抱いて赤く慟哭している

ラモウの人々が泣いている
水よりも貴重な娘たちがぶくぶく膨れて
全身で絶叫する声に
胸が張り裂ける

<訳注>
*ラモウ(拉孟):中国・雲南省とビルマ(現ミャンマー)との国境付近にある地名で、慰安婦施設のあった場所。

● 저자: 권순자

1958년 경상북도 경주에서 출생하였다. 경북대학교 사범대학 영어교육학과와 국민대학교 교육대학원 영어교육학과를 졸업했다.(석사논문명 『John Keats의 The fall of hyperion 연구 : 시인으로서의 성장과정』)

1986년 《포항문학》에 「사루비아」 외 2편으로 작품 활동을 시작하였으며, 2003년 《심상》 신인상을 수상했다. 시집으로 『바다로 간 사내』, 『우묵 횟집』, 『검은 늪』, 『낭만적인 악수』, 『붉은 꽃에 대한 명상』, 『순례자』 등이 있고, 『검은 늪』의 영역시집 『Mother's Dawn』이 있다.

2001년 시 「목련」으로 '동서커피문학상', 2003년 시 「장마」로 '시흥문학상', 2012년 시집 『붉은 꽃에 대한 명상』으로 '아르코 문학상'을 수상했다. 현재 서울 강신중학교 영어교사로 재직하고 있다.

일본대사관 앞에서 매주 열리는 '수요집회'에서 일본군 위안부 할머니들의 눈물 어린 증언을 직접 듣고, 그 분들을 위해 아무 것도 해드릴 수 없음을 통감하며 이 시대를 살아가는 양심으로서 실록을 겸한 일본군 위안부 시를 쓰게 되었다.

이메일 : 479sky@naver.com

● Author: Soonja Kwon

The poet, Soonja Kwon, was born in Gyeongju, North Gyeongsang Province, South Korea in 1958. She graduated from Kyungpook National University and Kookmin University Graduate School of Education with a major in English, submitting a theses entitled, "A Study of John Keats' *The Fall of Hyperion:* The growth process of the poet."

Her first published works were three poems, including "Sarubia" which appeared in *Pohang Literature* in 1986, and she received the New and Emerging Poet Award from *Shim Sang(Imagery)* in 2003. Her published books of poetry include *The Great Man who Went to Sea, Dream Another Sea-Umok Hoetjip(Umok Raw Fish Restaurant). Black Swamp*, Romantic Handshakes, Thoughts on Red Flowers, and Pilgrims-Splendor on the Prairie. Black Swamp has also been published in English, with the title *Mother's Dawn*.

Awards she has received include the East-West Coffee Literature Award for the poem "Magnolia" in 2001, the Siheung Literature Award for the poem "Rainy Season" in 2003 and the Arko Literature Award in 2012 for *Thoughts on Red Flowers*.

She is currently on the English faculty of Kangsin Middle school in Seoul.

After hearing the tearful stories of the old Korean women who were detained by the Japanese Army during World War II as "Comfort Women," at their Wednesday gatherings in front of the Japanese Embassy in Seoul where they hold in order to make their story known, protest their treatment and seek an apology from Japan, she felt she must do something for these women. As a result, she began to write poems portraying what they experienced as female slaves during the war, in the hopes that this would help the new generation to understand and remember what had occurred.

email : 479sky@naver.com

● 著者：權順慈（クォン・スンジャ）

1958年、慶尚北道慶州で生まれた。慶北大学師範大英語教育学科と国民大学教育大学院英語教育学科を卒業した。(修士論文名『John Keatsの The fall of hyperion 研究：詩人としての成長過程』)

1986年、《浦項文学》に「サルビア」外2篇を発表して、作品活動を始め、2003年、詩誌「心象」新人賞を受賞した。

詩集に『牛目(ウモク)刺身屋』、『黒い沼』、『ロマンチックな握手』、『赤い花に対する瞑想』、『巡礼者』』などがあり、『黒い沼』の英訳詩集として『Mother's Dawn』がある。

2001年、詩「木蓮」で「東西コーヒー文学賞」、2003年、詩「梅雨」で「始興文学賞」、2012年、詩集『赤い花に対する瞑想』で「アルコ文学賞」を受賞した。

現在、ソウルの江新(カンシン)中学校英語教師として在職中である。

日本大使館の前で毎週開かれる「水曜集会」で、元日本軍慰安婦たちの涙ぐましい証言を直接聞き、彼女たちのために何もして上げられないことを痛感しつつ、この時代を生きていく良心としての実録を兼ねた日本軍慰安婦の詩を綴った。

e-mail : 479sky@naver.com

● 일본어 번역 : 한 성 례

1955년 전북 정읍 출생. 세종대학교 일문과와 동 대학 정책과학대학원 국제지역학과 일본학 석사 졸업. 1986년 《시와 의식》 신인상으로 등단. 한국어 시집 『실험실의 미인』, 일본어 시집 『감색치마폭의 하늘은』, 『빛의 드라마』 등. '허난설헌문학상'과 일본에서 '시토소조상' 수상. 번역서 『세계가 만일 100명의 마을이라면』, 『붓다의 행복론』 등이 한국 중고등학교 각종 교과서의 여러 과목에 실렸으며, 마루야마 겐지의 『달에 울다』, 무라카미 류의 『한없이 투명에 가까운 블루』, 히가시노 게이고의 『백은의 잭』을 비롯하여 소설, 인문서, 에세이집 등 다수의 일본서적을 번역. 또한 잇시키 마코토의 『암호해독사』, 호소다 덴조의 『골짜기의 백합』, 고이케 마사요의 『동트기 전 한 시간』 등 일본 시집을 한국어로, 정호승의 『서울의 예수』, 김기택의 『바늘구멍 속의 폭풍』, 박주택의 『시간의 동공』, 안도현의 『얼음매미』 등 한국 시집을 일본어로 번역하는 등 한일 간에서 다수의 시집을 번역. 현재 세종사이버대학교 겸임교수.

● Japanese translation : **Sungrea Han**

Born in Jeong-eup, North Jeolla Province in 1955, Sungrea Han majored in Japanese Language and literature at Sejong University, and continued at the graduate school of Policy Science, completing a Master's degree in Japanology in the International Studies department. In 1986 she received the New and Emerging Poet Award from *Shim Sang (Imagery)*.

Her volumes of poems include *The Beauty of the Laboratory*, published in Korean and *The Sky is a Blue Skirt* and *Drama of Light* in Japanese. Her works have earned her the Heonan Seolheon Literature Award and Japan's Sitosozo Award. Many of her literary translations, including "What if the World Were a Village of 100 People" and "The Buddha Way to Happiness" have been published in middle and high school textbooks in Korea.

She has also translated Japanese novels to Korean, including *Crying at the Moon* by Maruyama Kenji, *Almost Transparent Blue* by Murakami Ryu and *The Silver Jack* by Higashino Keiko. In addition, she has translated numerous volumes of poetry from Japanese to Korean, including Isshiki Makoto's *The Codebreaker*, Hosoda Tenjo's *Lily of the Valley* and Koike Masayo's *One Hour Before Dawn*.

Poetry collections she has translated from Korean to Japanese include Jeong Ho-seung's *Jesus from Seoul*, Kim Ki-taek's *Storm in the Eye of a Needle*, Pak Ju-taek's *The Eyes of Time* and An Do-hyun's The Frozen Cicada. Currently, she is an adjunct professor at Sejong Cyber University.

● 日本文翻訳：**韓成禮（ハン・ソンレ）**

　1955年、韓国全羅北道井邑生まれ。世宗大学日語日文学科及び同大学政策科学大学院国際地域学科日本学修士卒業。1986年、「詩と意識」新人賞受賞で文壇デビュー。韓国語詩集『実験室の美人』、日本語詩集『柿色のチマ裾の空は』『光のドラマ』など。<許蘭雪軒文学賞>、<詩と創造賞>(日本)受賞。翻訳書『世界がもし100人の村だったら』、『ブッダの幸福論』などが韓国の中・高等学校の多様な科目の教科書に掲載された。丸山健二の『月に泣く』、村上龍の『限りなく透明に近いブルー』、東野圭吾の『白銀ジャック』をはじめとした日本の小説、エッセイ集、人文書などの多　数の日本書籍を韓国語に翻訳した。また、一色真理の『暗号解読手』、細田傳造の『谷間の百合』、小池昌代の『夜明け前一時間』などの日本の詩集を韓国語に、鄭浩承の『ソウルのイエス』、金基澤の『針穴の中の嵐』、朴柱澤の『時間の瞳孔』、安度眩の『氷蝉』などの韓国の詩集を日本語に翻訳するなど、日韓の間で詩集を多数翻訳した。現在、世宗サイバー大学兼任教授。

● 영문 번역：**앤 노드퀴스트**

　앤 노드퀴스트는 1958년 미국 코네티컷주 뉴헤이븐시에서 태어나 미국 동부에서 자랐다. 어린 시절 펜실베이니아주로 이사하여 거기에서 학교에 입학한 후 외국어에 관심이 생겼다. 고등학교와 오벌린(Oberlin)대학교에서 독어, 불어와 라틴어를 공부했다. 1990년부터 서울에 살면서 한국어와 일본어, 한자도 배우기 시작했다. 현재 남편, 딸과 함께 서울에서 살고 있다.
　현재 서울에서 편집자, 번역자로 일하고 있다.

● English translation：**Anne Nordquist**

　Anne Nordquist was born in 1958 in New Haven, Connecticut and grew up in the eastern United States, moving to Pennsylvania when she was very young. She developed an interested in foreign languages at a young age, studying German, French and Latin during high school and at Oberlin College. Later, when her job took her to Seoul, her interest in languages expanded with the study of Korean, Japanese and Chinese characters. She currently lives in Seoul with her husband and daughter, where she currently works as an editor and translator.

● 英文翻訳：**アン・ノードクイスト**

　アン・ノードクイストは、1958年、アメリカ合衆国コネチカット州のニューヘブン市で生まれ、アメリカのイーストコースト地域で育った。幼い頃にペンシルベニア州に移り住み、そこで学校に通いながら外国語に関心を持った。高校と大学(オーバリン大学)では、ドイツ語、フランス語、ラテン語を学んだ。1990年からソウルに在住し、韓国語と日本語、漢字なども学び始めた。現在は、夫、娘と共にソウルに暮らしながら、編集者、翻訳者としての仕事をしている。

「이 도서의 국립중앙도서관 출판예정도서목록(CIP)은 서지정보유통지원시스템 홈페이지(http://seoji.nl.go.kr)와 국가자료공동목록시스템(http://www.nl.go.kr/kolisnet)에서 이용하실 수 있습니다.(CIP제어번호: CIP2015029236)」

포엠포엠시인선 011

천개의 눈물
A Thousand Tears 一千粒の涙

권순자 한·영·일 대역 시집

초판 1쇄 발행 2015년 10월 26일

지은이	권순자
영문 번역자	앤 노드퀴스트(Anne Nordquist)
일본어 번역자	한성례(韓成禮)
기획·제작	한창옥 성국
디자인	성국
펴낸곳	도서출판 **포엠포엠 POEMPOEM**
출판등록	25100-2012-000083
본 사	서울시 송파구 잠실로 62 트리지움 308-1603 (05555)
편집실	부산시 해운대구 마린시티 3로 37 오르듀 1322호 (48118)
출간 문의	010-4563-0347, 02-413-7888 FAX. 051-911-3888
메 일	poempoem@hanmail.net
홈페이지	www.poempoem.kr
제작 및 공급처	산업디자인전문회사 두손컴

정가 10,000원

ISBN 979-11-86668-04-7   03810

저자와 협의 아래 인지를 생략합니다.
이 책의 저작권은 저자와 출판사에 있습니다.
저자 허락과 출판사 동의 없이 무단 전재 및 복제를 금합니다.
잘못 만들어진 책은 바꿔드립니다.

A Thousand Tears
POEMPOEM Poetry Collection 011

1st Print of 1st Edition October 26, 2015

Author Soonja Kwon

English translator Anne Nordquist

Japanese translator Sungrea Han

Executive Director Changok Han, Sunggook

Designer Sunggook

POEMPOEM Publisher

Registered publication 25100-2012-000083

Address 308-1603, Ill-Zium Apt., 62, Jamsil-ro, Songpa-gu, Seoul, Korea (05555)
1322, Ordew, 37, Marine city 3-ro, Haeundae-gu, Busan, Korea (48118)
Telephone (+82) 10-4563-0347, (+82) 2-413-7888 FAX. (+82) 51-911-3888
Email poempoem@hanmail.net
Website www.poempoem.kr

Production and supplier Industrial design company **Doosoncomm**

Price ₩10,000
ISBN 979-11-86668-04-7 03810

Copyright ⓒ 2015 **Soonja Kwon**
All Rights Reserved
No part of this book may be reproduced in any form without
written permission from the publisher.
Printed in the Republic of Korea